The Burden of Southern History

C. VANN WOODWARD

The Burden of Southern History

LOUISIANA STATE UNIVERSITY PRESS

BATON ROUGE

OTHER BOOKS BY C. VANN WOODWARD

Tom Watson: Agrarian Rebel
The Battle for Leyte Gulf
Reunion and Reaction
Origins of the New South
The Strange Career of Jim Crow

Preface

THE EXAMPLES SET BY OTHERS WHO HAVE ATTEMPTED TO
say why the heritage, or the collective character, or the
general outlook of a particular geographical grouping of
people is distinctive should constitute a warning to any
who are disposed to try again. Few such efforts have stood
up very well under the test of time. After a bit of aging,
the parochial point of view, the temporal bias, or the
didactic purpose begins to show through the pages more
and more. Authority and conviction seep out of the writing, and it is soon forgotten. While this is not true of
some efforts of the sort, it is true of a distressing proportion of them.

Perhaps the very nature of such enterprises makes for
ephemerality. They are without doubt surrounded by formidable hazards. The quality of distinctiveness is notori-
ously elusive and often changes markedly over the years,
sometimes under one's very eyes. Perhaps the most familiar
illustration of the ephemerality of the popular national
image is that of England since the sixteenth century. As

the image changed from Elizabethan to Puritan, to Restoration, to Georgian, to Victorian, to Edwardian, John Bull contrived to run through as many stereotyped personalities as an operatic tenor has roles and costumes. The possibilities for embarrassment to theorists of national character are obviously numerous. Those who had proved to their own satisfaction that insular isolation, Anglo-Saxon blood, or foggy weather determined the English character were left to contrive even more ingenious theories to explain why the geography, the blood, or the climate did not change with the personality, or why the same circumstances produced such a bewildering variety of results.

Efforts to substantiate the familiar claim of a distinctive Southern heritage and explain what produced it have traditionally relied rather strongly on circumstance or situation, policy or purpose of the Southern people. In such accounts natural forces or man's will figure largely. Much has been made of climate, for example, and its supposed effect upon speech, manners, architecture, habits of work, and style of living in the South. Climate was a special favorite of nineteenth-century European theorists, who were naturally interested in explaining or perhaps justifying the conduct and character of imperialist enterprises of their period. Since these adventures often took place in the tropics or in climates quite different from those of England and Western Europe, the emphasis on climate was understandable. But the same blinding tropical sun that so readily explained a peculiar pattern of imperialist institutions in the nineteenth century shines upon a quite different pattern of institutions in the twentieth century. So it is in the South, where new and radically different institutions, architecture, crops, and styles of living flourish in the same old climate, environed by the same old geography.

Other theorists made much of race, the racial composition of the people, or racial attitudes and policies of the dominant race toward the subordinate race. Some writers found an entirely adequate key to Southern identity and character in the white man's purpose of maintaining racial integrity or white supremacy. But of recent decades racial composition of the Southern population has altered appreciably because of migrations and other reasons, and racial purposes and policy have altered or swayed under new influences.

The better studies of group or national character in late years have tended to go beyond circumstance and purpose, beyond natural environment and public policy, and to stress *experience* as the influence of first importance. Their focus has been upon the impact of experience and how it has been translated into personality and group character. Much experience of importance is private and individual in nature and would in the main seem best left to the psychologist for study. The historian is more properly concerned with the public and external forces that go to make up the collective experience and give shape to the group character of a people.

The experience of the South is, of course, complex and varied. This book is concerned only with such experience as contributed to the molding of a distinctive heritage and only with certain selective aspects of that experience. The essays that make up this collection were written at different times for different purposes during the past eight years, all but two of them in the last four years. It is hoped, nevertheless, that all of them have something to contribute to an understanding of the collective experience and the distinctive character of the South.

The first and last of the essays, "The Search for Southern Identity" and "The Irony of Southern History," attack the question of what is peculiarly Southern more directly than do the others. "The Historical Dimension" turns to modern Southern letters for clues and definitions of the Southern heritage and its distinctiveness. In this and in all the essays the main comparison is with the North, or the non-Southern parts of America. The South is obviously American as well as Southern, and the first test of distinctiveness naturally lies in the establishment of a departure from the American norm.

The remaining essays deal with historical events or experiences that the South shared with the rest of America. But in each case the impact of the experience upon the South was markedly different from the impact registered upon other parts of the country. The Harpers Ferry Raid of 1859 was, to be sure, a national and not a regional event, and the prime movers, John Brown and his supporters, were about as Northern as they could well be. But the South's experience of that event was wholly different and distinct from that of the North. Similarly, the Civil War debate over equality for the Negro as "the third war aim," and the revolutionary aims framed for Reconstruction were of Northern origin, but the revolutionary impact of these movements and aims was very largely experienced in the South and not in the North. Likewise, the Populist movement was an event of national importance, but as a Southern experience it was largely felt as another alienation from the prevailing spirit in America. In these, as in other events, a common history has not necessarily meant a common experience, nor has it produced a uniformity of heritage and a conformity in character.

C. V. W.

Baltimore
May, 1960

Acknowledgments

THE ESSAYS IN THIS VOLUME, WITH ONE EXCEPTION, HAVE already appeared individually in various publications. The exception is "A Southern Critique for the Gilded Age," published here for the first time. Those previously published have been revised to some extent. In most cases, only a few words have been changed to eliminate anachronisms; in others, deletions have been made to remove allusions relevant only to the occasion on which the essay was delivered as a lecture. Also, in a few instances, changes have been made at the suggestion of friends to correct error or to clarify meaning. In no case, however, has the original intent of any essay been significantly altered.

For permission to reprint the essays that have already appeared I am grateful to the original publishers:

"The Search for Southern Identity" was first published in *The Virginia Quarterly Review*, XXXIV (1958), 321–38.

"The Historical Dimension" was first published in *The Virginia Quarterly Review*, XXXII (1956), 258–67.

"John Brown's Private War" was prepared for a lecture at Bennington College and published along with other lectures in the same series, edited by Daniel Aaron, *America in Crisis* (New York: Alfred A. Knopf, 1952).

"Equality: the Deferred Commitment" was delivered at the 125th Anniversary of the founding of Gettysburg College and published first in *The American Scholar,* XXVII (1958), 459–72.

"The Political Legacy of Reconstruction" was first published in *The Journal of Negro Education,* XXVI (1957), 231–40.

"The Populist Heritage and the Intellectual" was first published in *The American Scholar,* XXVIII (1959), 55–72.

"The Irony of Southern History" was a presidential address before the Southern Historical Association, published first in *The Journal of Southern History,* XIX (1953), 3–19, and later in Louis D. Rubin, Jr., and Robert D. Jacobs (eds.), *Southern Renascence* (Baltimore: The Johns Hopkins Press, 1953).

Contents

The Burden of Southern History

1

The Search for Southern Identity

THE TIME IS COMING, IF INDEED IT HAS NOT ALREADY arrived, when the Southerner will begin to ask himself whether there is really any longer very much point in calling himself a Southerner. Or if he does, he might well wonder occasionally whether it is worth while insisting on the point. So long as he remains at home where everybody knows him the matter hardly becomes an issue. But when he ventures among strangers, particularly up North, how often does he yield to the impulse to suppress the identifying idiom, to avoid the awkward subject, and to blend inconspicuously into the national pattern—to act the role of the standard American? Has the Southern heritage become an old hunting jacket that one slips on comfortably while at home but discards when he ventures abroad in favor of some more conventional or modish garb? Or is it perhaps an attic full of ancestral wardrobes useful only in connection with costume balls and play acting—staged primarily in Washington, D.C.?

Asking himself some similar questions about the New

England heritage, Professor George W. Pierson of Yale has come forth with some disturbing concessions about the integrity of his own region. Instead of an old hunting jacket, he suggests that we call New England "an old kitchen floor, now spatter-painted with many colors." He points out that roughly six out of every ten Connecticut "Yankees" are either foreign-born or born of foreign or mixed parentage, while only three have native forebears going as far back as two generations, and they are not necessarily New England forebears at that. "Like it or not," writes Pierson, "and no matter how you measure it—geographically, economically, racially or religiously, there is no New England Region today." It has become instead, he says, "an optical illusion and a land of violent contrast and change." And yet in spite of the wholesale and damaging concessions of his essay, which he calls "A Study in Denudation," he concludes that, "as a region of the heart and mind, New England is still very much alive."

One wonders if the Southerner, for his part, can make as many damaging admissions of social change and cultural erosion as our New England friend has made and come out with as firm a conclusion about the vitality of his own regional heritage. More doubt than assurance probably comes to mind at first. The South is still in the midst of an economic and social revolution that has by no means run its course, and it will not be possible to measure its results for a long time to come. This revolution has already leveled many of the old monuments of regional distinctiveness and may end eventually by erasing the very consciousness of a distinctive tradition along with the will to sustain it. The sustaining will and consciousness are also under the additional strain of a moral indictment against a discredited part of the tradition, an indictment more uncompromising than any since abolitionist times.

The Southerner may not have been very happy about many of those old monuments of regional distinctiveness that are now disappearing. He may, in fact, have deplored the existence of some—the one-horse farmer, one-crop agriculture, one-party politics, the sharecropper, the poll tax, the white primary, the Jim Crow car, the lynching bee. It would take a blind sentimentalist to mourn their passing. But until the day before yesterday there they stood, indisputable proof that the South was different. Now that they are vanished or on their way toward vanishing, we are suddenly aware of the vacant place they have left in the landscape and of our habit of depending upon them in final resort as landmarks of regional identification. To establish identity by reference to our faults was always simplest, for whatever their reservations about our virtues, our critics were never reluctant to concede us our vices and shortcomings.

It is not that the present South has any conspicuous lack of faults, but that its faults are growing less conspicuous and therefore less useful for purposes of regional identification. They are increasingly the faults of other parts of the country, standard American faults, shall we say. Many of them have only recently been acquired—could, in fact, only recently be afforded. For the great changes that are altering the cultural landscape of the South almost beyond recognition are not simply negative changes, the disappearance of the familiar. There are also positive changes, the appearance of the strikingly new.

The symbol of innovation is inescapable. The roar and groan and dust of it greet one on the outskirts of every Southern city. That symbol is the bulldozer, and for lack of a better name this might be called the Bulldozer Revolution. The great machine with the lowered blade symbolizes the revolution in several respects: in its favorite area of operation, the area where city meets country; in its relentless speed; in its supreme disregard for obstacles, its heedless methods; in what it demolishes and in what it builds. It is the advance agent of the metropolis. It encroaches upon rural life to expand urban life. It demolishes the old to make way for the new.

It is not the amount of change that is impressive about the Bulldozer Revolution so much as the speed and concentration with which it has come and with which it continues. In the decade of the forties, when urbanization was growing at a swift pace in the country as a whole, the cities of the South's fifty-three metropolitan areas grew more than three times as fast as comparable cities in the rest of the country, at a rate of 33.1 per cent as compared with 10.3 per cent elsewhere. For every three city dwellers in the South at the beginning of that decade there were four at the end, and for every five farm residents there were only four. An overwhelmingly rural South in 1930 had 5.5 millions employed in agriculture; by 1950, only 3.2 millions. A considerable proportion of these Southerners were moving directly from country to suburb, following the path of the bulldozer to "rurbanization" and skipping the phase of urbanization entirely. Rural Negroes, the most mobile of all Southerners, were more likely to move into the heart of the urban areas abandoned by the suburban dwellers. In the single decade of the forties the South lost a third of its rural-farm Negro population. If the same trend were continued through the present decade, it would reduce that part of the colored population to about one-fifth of the Negroes living in the region.

According to nearly all of the indices, so the economists find, economic growth of the South in recent years greatly exceeds the rate maintained in the North and East. The fact is the South is going through economic expansion and reorganization that the North and East completed a generation or more ago. But the process is taking place far more rapidly than it did in the North. Among all the many periods of change in the history of the South it is impossible to find one of such concentration and such substantive impact. The period of Reconstruction might appear a likely rival for this distinction, but that revolution was largely limited to changes in legal status and the ownership of property. The people remained pretty much where they were and continued to make their living in much the same way. All indications are that the bulldozer will leave a deeper mark upon the land than did the carpetbagger.

It is the conclusion of two Southern sociologists, John M. Maclachlan and Joe S. Floyd, Jr., that the present drive toward uniformity "with national demographic, economic, and cultural norms might well hasten the day when the South, once perhaps the most distinctively 'differ-

ent' American region, will have become in most such matters virtually indistinguishable from the other urban-
industrial areas of the nation."

The threat of becoming "indistinguishable," of being
submerged under a national steamroller, has haunted the
mind of the South for a long time. Some have seen it as
a menace to regional identity and the survival of a Southern heritage. Premonitions of the present revolution appeared during the industrial boom that followed the First
World War. Toward the end of the twenties two distinctive
attempts were made by Southerners to dig in and define
a perimeter of defense against further encroachment.

One of these entrenchments was that of the twelve
Southerners who wrote *I'll Take My Stand*. They sought
to define what they called "a Southern way of life against
what may be called the American or prevailing way," and
they agreed "that the best terms in which to represent
the distinction are contained in the phrase, Agrarian
versus Industrial." Agrarianism and its values were the
essence of the Southern tradition and the test of Southern
loyalty. Their credo held that "the whole way in which we
live, act, think, and feel," the humanist culture, "was
rooted in the agrarian way of life of the older South." They
called for "anti-industrial measures" which "might promise to stop the advances of industrialism, or even undo
some of them."

Even in 1930 the agrarians were prepared to admit "the
melancholy fact that the South itself has wavered a little
and shown signs of wanting to join up behind the common
or American industrial ideal." They admonished waverers

among the younger generation that the brave new South they contemplated would "be only an undistinguished replica of the usual industrial community."

Three decades later the slight "wavering" in the Southern ranks that disturbed the agrarians in 1930 would seem to have become a pell-mell rout. Defections came by the battalion. Whole regiments and armies deserted "to join up behind the common or American industrial ideal." In its pursuit of the American Way and the American Standard of Living the South was apparently doing all in its power to become what the agrarians had deplored as "only an undistinguished replica of the usual industrial community." The voice of the South in the 1950's had become the voice of the chamber of commerce, and Southerners appeared to be about as much absorbed in the acquirement of creature comforts and adult playthings as any other Americans. The twelve Southerners who took their stand in 1930 on the proposition that the Southern way stands or falls with the agrarian way would seem to have been championing a second lost cause. If they were right, then our questions would have already been answered, for the Southerner as a distinctive species of American would have been doomed, his tradition bereft of root and soil. The agrarian way contains no promise of continuity and endurance for the Southern tradition.

Two years before the agrarian pronouncement appeared, another attempt was made to define the essence of the Southern tradition and prescribe the test of Southern loyalty. The author of this effort was the distinguished historian, Professor Ulrich B. Phillips. His definition had no reference to economic institutions but was confined to a preoccupation with race consciousness. The essential theme of continuity and unity in the Southern heritage, wrote Professor Phillips, was "a common resolve indomitably maintained" that the South "shall be and remain a white man's country." This indomitable conviction could be "expressed with the frenzy of a demagogue or maintained with a patrician's quietude," but it was and had been from the beginning "the cardinal test of a Southerner and the central theme of southern history."

Professor Phillips' criterion of Southernism has proved somewhat more durable and widespread in appeal than that of the agrarians. It is not tied so firmly to an ephemeral economic order as was theirs. Nor does it demand—of the dominant whites, at least—any Spartan rejection of the flesh pots of the American living standard. Its adherents are able to enjoy the blessings of economic change and remain traditionalists at the same time. There are still other advantages in the Phillipsian doctrine. The traditionalist who has watched the Bulldozer Revolution plow under cherished old values of individualism, localism, family, clan, and rural folk culture has felt helpless and frustrated against the mighty and imponderable agents of change. Industrialism, urbanism, unionism, and big government conferred or promised too many coveted benefits. They divided the people and won support in the South, so that it was impossible to rally unified opposition to them.

The race issue was different. Advocates and agents of change could be denounced as outsiders, intruders, meddlers. Historic memories of resistance and cherished constitutional principles could be invoked. Racial prejudices, aggressions, and jealousies could be stirred to rally massive popular support. And with this dearly bought unity, which he could not rally on other issues, the frustrated traditionalist might at last take his stand for the defense of all the defiled, traduced, and neglected values of the traditional order. What then is the prospect of the Phillipsian "cardinal test" as a bulwark against change? Will it hold fast where other defenses have failed?

Recent history furnishes some of the answers. Since the last World War old racial attitudes that appeared more venerable and immovable than any other have exhibited a flexibility that no one would have predicted. One by one, in astonishingly rapid succession, many landmarks of racial discrimination and segregation have disappeared, and old barriers have been breached. Many remain, of course —perhaps more than have been breached—and distinctively Southern racial attitudes will linger for a long time. Increasingly the South is aware of its isolation in these attitudes, however, and is in defense of the institutions that embody them. They have fallen rapidly into discredit and under condemnation from the rest of the country and the rest of the world.

Once more the South finds itself with a morally discredited Peculiar Institution on its hands. The last time this happened, about a century ago, the South's defensive reaction was to identify its whole cause with the one institution that was most vulnerable and to make loyalty to an ephemeral aspect which it had once led in condemning

the cardinal test of loyalty to the whole tradition. Southerners who rejected the test were therefore forced to reject
the whole heritage. In many cases, if they were vocal in
their rejection, they were compelled to leave the South
entirely and return only at their peril. Unity was thus temporarily achieved, but with the collapse of the Peculiar
Institution the whole tradition was jeopardized and discredited for having been so completely identified with the
part abandoned.

Historical experience with the first Peculiar Institution
ought strongly to discourage comparable experiments with
the second. If Southernism is allowed to become identified
with a last ditch defense of segregation, it will increasingly
lose its appeal among the younger generation. Many will
be tempted to reject their entire regional identification,
even the name "Southern," in order to dissociate themselves from the one discredited aspect. If agrarianism has
proved to be a second lost cause, segregation is a likely
prospect for a third.

With the crumbling of so many defenses in the present,
the South has tended to substitute myths about the past.
Every self-conscious group of any size fabricates myths
about its past: about its origins, its mission, its righteousness, its benevolence, its general superiority. But few
groups in the New World have had their myths subjected
to such destructive analysis as those of the South have
undergone in recent years. While some Southern historians
have contributed to the mythmaking, others have been
among the leading iconoclasts, and their attacks have
spared few of the South's cherished myths.

The Cavalier Legend as the myth of origin was one of the earlier victims. The Plantation Legend of ante bellum grace and elegance has not been left wholly intact. The pleasant image of a benevolent and paternalistic slavery system as a school for civilizing savages has suffered damage that is probably beyond repair. Even the consoling security of Reconstruction as the common historic grievance, the infallible mystique of unity, has been rendered somewhat less secure by detached investigation. And finally, rude hands have been laid upon the hallowed memory of the Redeemers who did in the Carpetbaggers, and doubt has been cast upon the antiquity of segregation folkways. These faded historical myths have become weak material for buttressing Southern defenses, for time has dealt as roughly with them as with agrarianism and racism.

Would a hard-won immunity from the myths and illusions of Southern sectionalism provide some immunity to the illusions and myths of American nationalism? Or would the hasty divestment merely make the myth-denuded Southerner hasten to wrap himself in the garments of nationalism? The danger in the wholesale rejection of the South by the modern Southerner bent on reaffirming his Americanism is the danger of affirming more than he bargains for.

While the myths of Southern distinctiveness have been waning, national myths have been waxing in power and appeal. National myths, American myths have proved far more sacrosanct and inviolate than Southern myths. Millions of European immigrants of diverse cultural backgrounds have sought and found identity in them. The powerful urge among minority groups to abandon or disguise their distinguishing cultural traits and conform as quickly as possible to some national norm is one of the most familiar features in the sociology of American nationalism. European ethnic and national groups with traditions far more ancient and distinctive than those of the South have eagerly divested themselves of their cultural heritage in order to conform.

The conformist is not required nor expected to abandon his distinctive religion. But whether he remains a Protestant, a Catholic, or a Jew, his religion typically becomes subordinate or secondary to a national faith. Foreign observers have remarked that the different religions in America resemble each other more than they do their European counterparts. "By every realistic criterion," writes Will Herberg in his study of American religious sociology, "the American Way of Life is the operative faith of the American people." And where the mandates of the American Way of Life conflict with others, they take undisputed sway over the masses of all religions. Herberg describes it as "a faith that has its symbols and its rituals, its holidays and its liturgy, its saints and its sancta," and it is common to all Americans. "Sociologically, anthropologically, if one pleases," he writes, the American Way of Life "is the characteristic American religion, undergirding American life and overarching American society despite all indubitable differences of region, section, culture, and class." Differences such as those of region and section, "indubitable" though he admits them to be, he characterizes as "peripheral and obsolescent."

If the American Way of Life has become a religion, any deviation from it has become a sort of heresy. Regionalism in the typical American view is rather like the Turnerian frontier, a section on the move—or at least one that should keep moving, following a course that converges at not too remote a point with the American Way. It is a season's halt of the American caravan, a temporary encampment of an advancing society, eternally on the move toward some undefined goal of progress. If the encampment of regionalism threatens to entrench or dig in for a permanent stand, it comes to be regarded as "peripheral and obsolescent," an institutionalized social lag.

The same urge to conformity that operates upon ethnic or national minorities to persuade them to reject identification with their native heritage or that of their forebears operates to a degree upon the Southerner as well. Since the cultural landscape of his native region is being altered almost beyond recognition by a cyclone of social change, the Southerner may come to feel as uprooted as the immigrant. Bereft of his myths, his peculiar institutions, even his familiar regional vices, he may well reject or forget his regional identification as completely as the immigrant.

Is there nothing about the South that is immune from the disintegrating effect of nationalism and the pressure for conformity? Is there not something that has not changed? There is only one thing that I can think of, and that is its history. By that I do not mean a Southern brand of Shintoism, the worship of ancestors. Nor do I mean written history and its interpretation, popular and mythical, or professional and scholarly, which have changed often and will change again. I mean rather the collective experience of the Southern people. It is in just this respect that the South remains the most distinctive region of the country. In their unique historic experience as Americans the Southerners should not only be able to find the basis for continuity of their heritage but also make contributions that balance and complement the experience of the rest of the nation.

At this point the risks of our enterprise multiply. They are the risks of spawning new myths in place of the old. Awareness of them demands that we redouble precautions and look more cautiously than ever at generalizations.

To start with a safe one, it can be assumed that one of the most conspicuous traits of American life has been its economic abundance. From early colonial days the fabulous riches of America have been compared with the scarcity and want of less favored lands. Immense differentials in economic welfare and living standards between the United States and other countries still prevail. In an illuminating book called *People of Plenty*, David Potter persuasively advances the thesis that the most distinguishing traits of national character have been fundamentally shaped by the abundance of the American living standard. He marshals evidence of the effect that plenty has had upon such decisive phases of life as the nursing and training of babies, opportunities for education and jobs, ages of marriage and childbearing. He shows how abundance has determined characteristic national attitudes between parents and children, husband and wife, superior and subordinate, between one class and another, and how it has

molded our mass culture and our consumer oriented society. American national character would indeed appear
inconceivable without this unique experience of abundance.

The South at times has shared this national experience
and, in very recent years, has enjoyed more than a taste of
it. But the history of the South includes a long and quite
un-American experience with poverty. So recently as 1938,
in fact, the South was characterized by the President as
"The Nation's Economic Problem No. 1." And the problem was poverty, not plenty. It was a poverty emphasized
by wide regional discrepancies in living standard, per
capita wealth, per capita income, and the good things that
money buys, such as education, health, protection, and the
many luxuries that go to make up the celebrated American
Standard of Living. This striking differential was no temporary misfortune of the great depression but a continuous and conspicuous feature of Southern experience since
the early years of the Civil War. During the last half of
the nineteenth and the first half of the twentieth centuries,
when technology was multiplying American abundance
with unprecedented rapidity, the South lagged far behind.
In 1880 the per capita wealth of the South, based on esti-
mated true valuation of property, was $376 as compared
with $1,186 per capita in the states outside the South. In
the same year the per capita wealth of the South was 27
per cent of that of the Northeastern states. That was just
about the same ratio contemporaneously existing between
the per capita wealth of Russia and that of Germany.

Generations of scarcity and want constitute one of the
distinctive historical experiences of the Southern people,

an experience too deeply embedded in their memory to be wiped out by a business boom and too deep not to admit of some uneasiness at being characterized historically as a "People of Plenty." That they should have been for so long a time a "People of Poverty" in a land of plenty is one mark of enduring cultural distinctiveness. In a nation known around the world for the hedonistic ethic of the American Standard of Living, the Southern heritage of scarcity remains distinctive.

A closely related corollary of the uniquely American experience of abundance is the equally unique American experience of success. During the Second World War Professor Arthur M. Schlesinger made an interesting attempt to define the national character, which he brought to a close with the conclusion that the American character "is bottomed upon the profound conviction that nothing in the world is beyond its power to accomplish." In this he gave expression to one of the great American legends, the legend of success and invincibility. It is a legend with a foundation in fact, for much can be adduced from the American record to support it and explain why it has flourished. If the history of the United States is lacking in some of the elements of variety and contrast demanded of any good story, it is in part because of the very monotonous repetition of successes. Almost every major collective effort, even those thwarted temporarily, succeeded in the end. American history *is* a success story. Why should such a nation not have a "profound conviction that nothing in the world is beyond its power to accomplish"? Even the hazards of war—including the prospect of war against an unknown enemy with untried weapons—proves no exception to the rule. The advanced science and weaponry of the Russian challenger are too recent to have registered their impact on the legend. The American people have never known the chastening experience of being on the losing side of a war. They have, until very recently, solved every major problem they have confronted—or had it solved for them by a smiling fortune. Success and victory are still national habits of mind.

This is but one among several American legends in which the South can participate only vicariously or in part. Again the Southern heritage is distinctive. For Southern history, unlike American, includes large components of frustration, failure, and defeat. It includes not only an overwhelming military defeat but long decades of defeat in the provinces of economic, social, and political life. Such a heritage affords the Southern people no basis for the delusion that there is nothing whatever that is beyond their power to accomplish. They have had it forcibly and repeatedly borne in upon them that this is not the case. Since their experience in this respect is more common among the general run of mankind than that of their fellow Americans, it would seem to be a part of their heritage worth cherishing.

American opulence and American success have combined to foster and encourage another legend of early origin, the legend of American innocence. According to this legend Americans achieved a sort of regeneration of sinful man by coming out of the wicked Old World and removing to an untarnished new one. By doing so they shook off the wretched evils of feudalism and broke free from tyranny, monarchism, aristocracy, and privilege— all those institutions which, in the hopeful philosophy of the Enlightenment, accounted for all, or nearly all, the evil in the world. The absence of these Old World ills in America, as well as the freedom from much of the injustice and oppression associated with them, encouraged a singular moral complacency in the American mind. The self-image implanted in Americans was one of innocence as compared with less fortunate people of the Old World. They were a chosen people and their land a Utopia on the make. Alexis de Tocqueville's patience was tried by this complacency of the American. "If I applaud the freedom which its inhabitants enjoy, he answers, 'Freedom is a fine thing, but few nations are worthy to enjoy it.' If I remark on the purity of morals which distinguishes the United States," complained Tocqueville, " 'I can imagine,' says he, 'that a stranger, who has been struck by corruption of all other nations, is astonished at the difference.' "

How much room was there in the tortured conscience of the South for this national self-image of innocence and moral complacency? Southerners have repeated the American rhetoric of self admiration and sung the perfection of American institutions ever since the Declaration of Independence. But for half that time they lived intimately with a great social evil and the other half with its aftermath. It was an evil that was even condemned and abandoned by the Old World, to which America's moral superiority was supposedly an article of faith. Much of the South's intellectual energy went into a desperate effort to convince the world that its peculiar evil was actually a "positive good," but it failed even to convince itself. It writhed in the torments of its own conscience until it plunged into catastrophe to escape. The South's preoccupation was with guilt, not with innocence, with the reality of evil, not with the dream of perfection. Its experience in this respect, as in several others, was on the whole a thoroughly un-American one.

An age-long experience with human bondage and its evils and later with emancipation and its shortcomings did not dispose the South very favorably toward such popular American ideas as the doctrine of human perfectibility, the belief that every evil has a cure, and the notion that every human problem has a solution. For these reasons the utopian schemes and the gospel of progress that flourished above the Mason and Dixon Line never found very wide acceptance below the Potomac during the nineteenth century. In that most optimistic of centuries in the most optimistic part of the world, the South remained basically pessimistic in its social outlook and its moral philosophy. The experience of evil and the experience of tragedy are parts of the Southern heritage that are as difficult to reconcile with the American legend of innocence and social felicity as the experience of poverty and defeat are to reconcile with the legends of abundance and success.

One of the simplest but most consequential generalizations ever made about national character was Tocqueville's that America was "born free." In many ways that is the basic distinction between the history of the United States and the history of other great nations. We skipped the feudal stage, just as Russia skipped the liberal stage. Louis Hartz has pointed up the complex consequences for the history of American political thought. To be a conservative and a traditionalist in America was a contradiction in terms, for the American Burke was forever conserving John Locke's liberalism, his only real native tradition. Even the South, in its great period of reaction against Jefferson, was never able fully to shake off the grip of Locke and its earlier self-image of liberalism. That is why its most original period of theoretical inspiration, the "Reactionary Enlightenment," left almost no influence upon American thought.

There is still a contribution to be derived from the South's un-American adventure in feudal fantasy. While the South was not born Lockean, it went through a Lockean phase in its youth. But as Hartz admits, it was "an alien child in a liberal family, tortured and confused, driven to a fantasy life." There *are* Americans, after all, who were not "born free." They are also Southerners. They have yet to achieve articulate expression of their uniquely un-American experience. This is not surprising, since white Southerners have only recently found expression of the tragic potentials of their past in literature. The Negro has yet to do that. His first step will be an acknowledgment that he is also a Southerner as well as an American.

One final example of a definition of national character to which the South proves an exception is an interesting one by Thornton Wilder. "Americans," says Mr. Wilder, "are abstract. They are disconnected. They have a relation, but it is to everywhere, to everybody, and to always." This quality of abstraction he finds expressed in numerous ways —in the physical mobility of Americans, in their indifference or, as he might suggest, their superiority to place, to locality, to environment. "For us," he writes, "it is not *where* genius lived that is important. If Mount Vernon and Monticello were not so beautiful in themselves and relatively accessible, would so many of us visit them?" he asks. It is not the concrete but the abstract that captures the imagination of the American and gives him identity, not the here-and-now but the future. " 'I am I,' he says, 'because my plans characterize me.' Abstract! Abstract!" Mr. Wilder's stress upon abstraction as an American characteristic recalls what Robert Penn Warren in a different connection once described as "the fear of abstraction" in the South, "the instinctive fear, on the part of black or white, that the massiveness of experience, the concreteness of life, will be violated; the fear of abstraction."

According to Mr. Wilder, "Americans can find in environment no confirmation of their identity, try as they may." And again, "Americans are disconnected. They are exposed to all place and all time. No place nor group nor movement can say to them: we are waiting for you; it is right for you to be here." The insignificance of place, locality, and community for Thornton Wilder contrasts strikingly with the experience of Eudora Welty of Mississippi. "Like a good many other [regional] writers," she says, "I am myself touched off by place. The place where I am and the place I know, and other places that familiarity with and love for my own make strange and lovely and enlightening to look into, are what set me to writing my stories." To her, "place opens a door in the mind," and she speaks of "the blessing of being located—contained."

To do Mr. Wilder justice, he is aware that the Southern states constitute an exception to his national character of abstraction, "enclaves or residual areas of European feeling," he calls them. "They were cut off, or resolutely cut themselves off, from the advancing tide of the country's modes of consciousness. Place, environment, relations, repetitions are the breath of their being."

The most reassuring prospect for the survival of the South's distinctive heritage is the magnificent body of literature produced by its writers in the last three decades —the very years when the outward traits of regional distinctiveness were crumbling. The Southern literary renaissance has placed its writers in the vanguard of national letters and assured that their works will be read as long as American literature is remembered. The distinguishing feature of the Southern school, according to Allen Tate, is "the peculiar historical consciousness of the Southern writer." He defines the literary renaissance as "a literature conscious of the past in the present." The themes that have inspired the major writers have not been the flattering myths nor the romantic dreams of the South's past. Disdaining the polemics of defense and justification, they have turned instead to the somber realities of hardship and defeat and evil and "the problems of the human heart in conflict with itself." In so doing they have brought to realization for the first time the powerful literary potentials of the South's tragic experience and heritage. Such comfort as they offer lies, in the words of William Faulkner, in reminding us of "the courage and honor and hope and pride and compassion and pity and sacrifice" with which man has endured.

After Faulkner, Wolfe, Warren, and Welty no literate Southerner could remain unaware of his heritage or doubt its enduring value. After this outpouring it would seem more difficult than ever to deny a Southern identity, to be "merely American." To deny it would be to deny our history. And it would also be to deny to America participation in a heritage and a dimension of historical experience that America very much needs, a heritage that is far more closely in line with the common lot of mankind than the national legends of opulence and success and innocence. The South once thought of itself as a "peculiar people," set apart by its eccentricities, but in many ways modern America better deserves that description.

The South was American a long time before it was Southern in any self-conscious or distinctive way. It remains more American by far than anything else, and has all along. After all, it fell the lot of one Southerner from Virginia to define America. The definition he wrote in 1776 voiced aspirations that were rooted in his native region before the nation was born. The modern Southerner should be secure enough in his national identity to escape the compulsion of less secure minorities to embrace uncritically all the myths of nationalism. He should be secure enough also not to deny a regional heritage because it is at variance with national myth. It is a heritage that should prove of enduring worth to him as well as to his country.

2

The Historical Dimension

IT WOULD SEEM TO BE HIGH TIME FOR SOME SOUTHERN
historian to abandon temporarily the standoffishness of
his guild and make his bow to Southern men of letters.
Not that it is necessary at this late date to acknowledge
that the literary men have earned the greater acclaim and
distinction. That goes without saying. What is really
needed is some acknowledgment of the genuine debt the
historians owe to the poets, playwrights, and novelists—
particularly the novelists—as well as an acknowledgement
of vital relations between the crafts.

The generation of Southerners who went to college in
the 1920's usually took a defensive attitude toward the
history of their region, or affected indifference. It was an
attitude compounded of several factors: the college boy's
revolt against the ideas and values of his parents, the striv-
ing to cover up a consciousness of provincialism, and an
eagerness to appear abreast of the times, if not a little in
advance. Even so staunch a traditionalist as Donald Davidson admitted the force of these impulses when he wrote

in 1926: "The gallantries of the Lost Cause, the legends of Southern history—these he may admire, but they came to him mouthed over and cheapened . . . the treacly lamentations of the old school."

Being "old school" in the 1920's was the worst possible offense against the canons of the collegian, and he strove with all his might to avoid the charge. He readily gathered from the literary monitors of fashion and taste whom he admired that there was nothing issuing from his native region in the way of arts and letters that was worth his notice. When *The Sound and the Fury* appeared in 1929, the young Southerner was assured by the *New Republic* that it "signified nothing." He also absorbed the impression from numerous quarters that the history of the South was generally discreditable, if not faintly ridiculous. All things considered, it was not the most auspicious background for one who aspired to become a Southern historian.

The Southerner who was graduated from college about 1930 was soon aware of new voices in the land and new forces astir. He doubtless derived some encouragement from the contemporary awakening of historical scholarship, particularly if he hoped to be a historian. But it was soon apparent that the stir among historians was only a minor aspect of a wider intellectual awakening in the South. The most brilliant manifestation was in the field of letters and literary criticism. To mention only a few books of one author, within the three years beginning in 1929 there appeared William Faulkner's *Sartoris, The Sound and the Fury, As I Lay Dying, Sanctuary,* and

Light in August—a one-man renaissance by 1932. Katherine Anne Porter's first book, *Flowering Judas,* appeared in 1930. Shortly before that, there arose the bright star of Thomas Wolfe with the appearance of *Look Homeward, Angel.* Of all American novels, that is the book of the young man, especially the young Southerner, and no one who read it in his youth will forget the strange excitement of the experience. The early thirties were stirring years to be discovering the South and its history and spending the years of one's youth.

The spice of controversy and polemic was added by the Nashville manifesto, *I'll Take My Stand,* in 1930. Counterblast provoked counterblast, and the controversy raged on in the pages of Davidson's *Attack on Leviathan* and in successive numbers of the *American Review* and later in the *Southern Review.* With the establishment of the latter in 1935 the center of the avant garde of American literary criticism shifted temporarily to the banks of the Mississippi at Baton Rouge. Gradually the pundits and critical moguls on the Hudson began to alter their tone about the "Sahara of the Bozart." An occasional note of praise, then of cautious respect, was succeeded by fulsome acclaim and eventually by a sort of awed puzzlement at this sudden flowering of the cultural desert. The young Southerner took a vicarious pride in all this achievement, a pride that did wonders for his provincial inferiority complex. He hailed the new names as they appeared—Robert Penn Warren, Eudora Welty, Tennessee Williams—and new ones kept arriving on the scene.

Allen Tate spoke of this outpouring as "quite temporary"

in 1935 and thought that year marked "the height of the
Southern literary renaissance." But in 1935 some of the
brighter luminaries had not yet appeared on the horizon.
Again, in 1945, Tate wrote that "that Renascence is over."
But in 1955 Andrew Nelson Lytle could declare: "The
Renascence has been going on for thirty years with little
sign of diminishment." The fact is that we have grown up
with this movement, and it will remain for a later generation to fix its limits and assess its achievements.

Our concern here is with its significance for the historian rather than with its place in history. It was early
apparent that the new Southern writers had something
special to say to the historian, something that no other
living American writers—and few dead ones—seemed to
say. If he had read any American literature in college,
it was not likely to have been of Southern origin. The
literary awakening of the Middle West was still in the
public eye in the twenties, and the collegian of that era
plowed through his Theodore Dreiser, Edgar Lee Masters, Sherwood Anderson, and Sinclair Lewis. There was
little in their pages to increase his respect or deepen his
appreciation for the uses of history. The characters in the
novels of Dreiser, Anderson, and Lewis appear on the
scene from nowhere, trailing no clouds of history, dis-
sociated from the past. They seem to have left it behind
them in New England, or Norway, or Bavaria, and along
with their past they checked their forebears, their historical
roots and associations. One has the feeling that they considered that heritage a good riddance. They rarely dis-
cuss it, and one gathers there was no room for it in such

baggage as they brought along to Gopher Prairie, Winesburg, or Chicago.

In the work of some later writers the historical perspective is even more flat. Hemingway's characters appear to live completely in the present. To emphasize their historical rootlessness they are invariably pictured as expatriates, as wanderers, as soldiers or adventurers. They are temporarily in Italy or Spain, in France or Africa, in Cuba or the Florida Keys. A Hemingway hero with a grandfather is inconceivable, and he is apparently quite as bereft of uncles, aunts, cousins, and in-laws, not to mention neighbors and poor relations. With Dos Passos the story is somewhat different. But for all his marvelous gift for evoking a given place or a period of the recent past (a gift historians can but envy), his characters are exclusively preoccupied with personal problems or with social problems of their own time. They are haunted by no ghosts of the past, and the past does not seem to be part of the present. If our collegian was coached through a reading of the literary flowering of New England that took place a century or more ago, he will have discovered little more of the historical dimension than he found in the more recent schools. The New Englanders, with the exception of Hawthorne, regularly pictured the individual starkly alone with his problems, his wilderness, or his God. Cooper and Henry James offer a certain amount of historical depth, but the characters of Melville appear to live entirely in the present or the future and to concern themselves seldom with the past.

To discover the new school of Southern fiction after

1930 was to enter suddenly upon a new world of the imagination, a world in which the historical imagination played a supreme part. In his essay on "The Profession of Letters in the South," Allen Tate has fixed upon "the peculiarly historical consciousness of the Southern writer" as the secret spring of creative energies that has fed the whole literary movement in the South during the last three decades. Tate has also suggested an historical explanation for the intellectual awakening of the South and the heightening of historical consciousness so characteristic of it. He suggests that after the First World War the South arrived at a crossroads of history where an old traditional order was being rapidly obliterated and a new modern order was being simultaneously brought to birth. Caught at these crossroads, the Southerner was made more keenly conscious at once of the present and of the past. His sensitivity to the current change heightened his awareness of past differences, and his intensified remembrance of things past added corresponding poignancy to his awareness of things present. As Tate put it, "that backward glance gave us the Southern renascence, a literature conscious of the past in the present."

A claim to what Tate called "the peculiarly historical consciousness of the Southern writer" was made by Ellen Glasgow in her posthumously published autobiography. "I had been born," she wrote, "with an intimate feeling for the spirit of the past, and the lingering poetry of time and place." In the last volume of his ten-volume work, Arnold Toynbee advances the theory that "the vividness of historical impressions is apt to be proportionate to their violence and painfulness" and speculates that "a child who had lived through the American Civil War in the territory of the Southern Confederacy would be likely to grow up more historical-minded than one who had lived through the same experience at the North." In this connection a statement of Katherine Anne Porter has some relevance. "I am a grandchild of a lost War," she writes in *The Days Before,* "and I have blood-knowledge of what life can be in a defeated country on the bare bones of privation."

In emphasizing the place that historical consciousness plays in contemporary Southern writing, I have no reference to the vogue of the conventional historical novel. The South has produced its share of the historical romance, and during the early years of the present century when the market reached one of its peaks, Southern popular writers produced considerably more than their share of best-sellers. But production figures reveal no particular regional concentration. The Northern and Western writers have proved themselves as handy at this craft as the Southern. Their product has little to do with Tate's "literature conscious of the past in the present." And it might be observed parenthetically that modern craftsmen of that school sometimes reverse Tate's description and tend at times to interject a dubious awareness of the present in the past. At any rate, we are not concerned here with the historical romance—whether its purpose is to score some point about the present or to settle some score about the past.

It is interesting but quite tangential to the argument that

the first books of two leading figures of the Southern
Renaissance were not in the field of fiction but of history.
These were Allen Tate's biography of Stonewall Jackson,
published in 1928, and Robert Penn Warren's biography
of John Brown, published in 1929. It is also a source of
great fascination to the historian—though still neither
essential nor quite relevant to the thesis—that some of
our most gifted novelists have chosen historical periods or
figures or movements as subjects. Ellen Glasgow set out
early in her career to write what she described as "a social
history of Virginia" from 1850 to 1912. It must be admitted, however, that none of her "Novels of the Com-
monwealth," as she called them, are among her best
works. Faulkner has been engaged for the better part of
three decades in rounding out his Yoknapatawpha world
of McCaslins, Sartorises, and Compsons; its MacCallums,
Bundrens, and Snopeses; its Joe Christmases, Lucas Beau-
champs, and Charles Bons. While this saga so far represents the supreme creation of the Southern Renaissance,
it is not history in any usual sense. And it is not unlikely
that the Faulkner critics have gone astray in thinking
of the Yoknapatawpha novels as Southern history in micro-
cosm, or as representing any very consistent ideas or theories about Southern history. In the universality of their
meaning they are more, and in their immediate application
less, than that.

The Southern novelist who comes nearest approaching an historical subject after the manner of an historian
is Warren. Yet Warren is careful and perfectly correct to
warn the reader of *Night Rider* that "although this book

was suggested by certain events which took place in Kentucky in the early years of the century, it is not, in any strict sense, a historical novel." What Warren has pronounced "the boneheadedness or gospel-bit hysteria" of those who insist upon making either history or a political tract out of *All the King's Men* drives the author to despair. He quotes Louis Armstrong as remarking, "There is some folks that if they don't know, you can't tell 'em." While Warren selects the same sort of subject matter as the historian—the Black Patch War in Kentucky during the first decade of the century, a financial tycoon of Tennessee in the twenties, or a demagogue of Louisiana in the thirties —he could rightly say of them all, as he said of the first, that they are not historical novels in any strict sense. At the same time it could be as accurately said that they quicken and vivify our consciousness of history in a way that conventional historical novels, as well as many bona fide histories, do not.

The relevance of the theme of "historical consciousness" in Southern letters would have been the same had the novelists never tackled a historical subject or treated any period prior to Appomattox. It is not the period nor the subject that is the point but, in Tate's words, the consciousness of the past in the present. Here, among many possible illustrations, one thinks of Katherine Anne Porter's Miranda in *Old Mortality,* seeking through the years of her youth to find and come to terms with her family's past and her own past and to relate them to the present. Or of Thomas Wolfe's Eugene Gant, "the haunter of himself, trying for a moment to recover what he had been part of . . . a stone, a leaf, an unfound door," and lyrically imploring, "Ghost, come back again." Or of Faulkner's Quentin Compson in *Absalom, Absalom!* groping through the convolutions of Colonel Sutpen's incredible legend for an answer to Shreve McCannon's questions in 1910. Or of Warren's Jack Burden in *All the King's Men* brooding endlessly over the faded letters and diaries of Cass Mastern for a lost meaning to the past and a key to the present in the 1930's.

This preoccupation, this almost obsessive concern of Southern writers with the past in the present has been expressed often explicitly as well as implicitly in their stories. Thus John Peale Bishop wrote in his essay, "The South and Tradition," that "without a past we are living not in the present, but in a vague and rather unsatisfactory future." Katherine Anne Porter remarks of Miranda's family that "their hearts and imaginations were captivated by their past," but while the author never treats that past as such, it is constantly obtruding itself into the present she does treat. On the other hand, Ellen Glasgow did repeatedly treat historical episodes and epochs, but her most successful use of the past was probably in such unhistorical novels as *Barren Ground* and *The Sheltered Life.* For all his reference to the Old South, Faulkner has never attempted a full-bodied treatment of the Civil War, as much as it impinges on his major themes. His themes have been preponderantly those of the post bellum South. Still, he has Gavin Stevens say in *Intruder in the Dust,* "The past is never dead. It's not even past." In the course of a bear hunt we are taken all the way back to tribal

life among the aborigines of Mississippi through Sam Fathers, their descendant. For the Southern school the present
is a fleeting segment of the cumulative past and might be
described by the concluding words of *All the King's Men:*
". . . out of history, into history and the awful responsibility of Time."

Another deeply embedded trait of the Southern novelists that has strong appeal to the historian is their way of
treating man not as an individual alone with his conscience or his God, as the New Englanders were inclined
to do, or alone at sea with a whale or a marlin, or alone
in a ring with a bull, but as an inextricable part of a living history and community, attached and determined in
a thousand ways by other wills and destinies of people
he has only heard about. Herbert Marshall McLuhan has
remarked that "the sense of belonging to a great chain of
persons and events, passive yet responsible, is everywhere
in Faulkner." And he quotes T. S. Stribling on "the chain
of wrongs and violences out of which his life had been
molded." In *Band of Angels* Warren has its narrator say,
"You live through time, that little piece of time that is
yours, but that piece of time is not only your own life, it is
the summing-up of all the other lives that are simultaneous
with yours." This, in sum, is also the way the historian
tries to see the individual and the forces that mold him.

Francis B. Simkins has urged that "the historian of the
South should join the social novelist who accepts the values
of the age and section about which he writes." The trouble
lies in the ambiguities of the verb "to accept." And there is
also the question of which values and what age. Faulkner

certainly never accepted the values of the Snopeses, nor of the Compsons either. For it is just the tragedy of the Compsons in *The Sound and the Fury* that in the person of Jason Compson they *did* accept the values of the age —the age of the Snopeses. The historian like the novelist should not change his values with his ages, whether it is the age of Colonel Sutpen or of Jason Compson. This was precisely the mistake of the John B. Gordons and Basil Dukes and their generation. They did.

The best of the Southern novelists have never set out to defend the values or the prejudices or the errors of any particular age or section. It is true that their books are often filled with tales of horror and lust and betrayal and degradation. But they have not paused to reckon their popularity in attacking the values of their own age or any other. They have not set up as defenders of a cause, either one lost or one still sought. They have proved themselves able to confront the chaos and irony of history with the admission that they can fit them into no neat pattern and explain them by no pat theory.

The historian is fortunate, I think, in sharing a period with literary men of great talent who share so many of his own values, so much of his own outlook and point of view, and so much of his own subject matter. He can afford to take pride in their achievements and comfort in their example. This is no plea for the relaxation of the severe limitations of the historian's discipline, nor for his borrowing the novelist's license. But once the historian abandons an old and false analogy with the natural sciences and sees that his craft employs no special concepts nor categories nor special terminology, he will admit that he attempts to "explain" history in the same way he explains events in ordinary life—his own as well as that of his fellow men—and with much the same language, moral and psychological. He should then acknowledge that Southern men of letters have advanced many of the aims he shares. They have helped us penetrate the romantic haze of an older generation as well as the cynical stereotypes of our own. They have endowed the denigrated and emotionally impoverished New South with a sense of tragedy and dignity that history had hitherto reserved for the Old Régime, and they have enriched our consciousness of the past in the present. They have helped to bring the Negro into intelligible focus without the glasses of sentimentality. And they have given history meaning and value and significance as events never do merely because they happen. These are things the historian also strives to do, and he should seek to do them with the same fortitude and honesty.

3

John Brown's Private War

THE FIGURE OF JOHN BROWN IS STILL WRAPPED IN OBSCUR-
ity and myth. In the fourteen biographies of Brown published since 1859, the legend makers have done their part,
but much of the difficulty is inherent in the nature of
Brown's life and character. His fifty-nine years were divided sharply into two periods. The obscurity of his first
fifty-five years was of the sort natural to a humble life
unassociated with events of importance. The obscurity of
his last four years, filled with conspiratorial activities, was
in large part the deliberate work of Brown, his fellow
conspirators, and their admirers.

Poverty and failure haunted the first fifty-five years of
John Brown's life. The father of twenty children, he was
compelled to see his family drag along in want and at
times in something approaching destitution. In thirty-five
years he was engaged in more than twenty different business ventures in six states. Most of them ended in failure,
some in bankruptcy, and at least two in crime. Brown was
involved for years as defendant in one litigation after an-

other brought against him for failure to meet his financial obligations. "Several of the cases in question leave no doubt of flagrant dishonesty on his part in both business and family relations," concludes Professor James C. Malin. The historian suggests that "this record of unreliability proven in court" might serve as "an index to the reliability of John Brown as a witness after he became a public character." The remarkable thing about this record is that it seems to have interfered in no way with the second of his careers. After 1855 John Brown abandoned his unprofitable business career when he was almost penniless and for the rest of his life was without remunerative employment. He depended for support upon donations from people whom he convinced of his integrity and reliability. Here and elsewhere there is strong evidence that Brown was somehow able to inspire confidence and intense personal loyalty.

The Kansas phase of Brown's guerrilla warfare has given rise to the "Legend of Fifty-six," a fabric of myth that has been subjected to a more rigorous examination than any other phase of Brown's life has ever received. Malin establishes beyond question that "John Brown did not appear to have had much influence either in making or marring Kansas history," that his exploits "brought tragedy to innocent settlers," but that "in no place did he appear as a major factor." He also establishes a close correlation between the struggle over freedom and slavery and local clashes over conflicting land titles on the Kansas frontier, and he points out that "the business of stealing horses under the cloak of fighting for freedom and running them off to the Nebraska-Iowa border for sale" is a neglected aspect of the struggle for "Bleeding Kansas." John Brown and his men engaged freely and profitably in this business and justified their plunder as the spoils of war. Two covenants that Brown drew up for his followers contained a clause specifically providing for the division of captured property among the members of his guerrilla band.

It would be a gross distortion, however, to dismiss John Brown as a frontier horse thief. He was much too passionately and fanatically in earnest about his war on slavery to permit of any such oversimplification. His utter fearlessness, courage, and devotion to the cause were greatly admired by respectable antislavery men who saw in the old Puritan an ideal revolutionary leader.

One exploit of Brown in Kansas, however, would seem to have put him forever beyond the pale of association with intelligent opponents of slavery. This was the famous Pottawatomie massacre of May 24, 1856. John Brown, leading four of his sons, a son-in-law, and two other men, descended by night upon an unsuspecting settlement of four proslavery families. Proceeding from one home to another the raiders took five men out, murdered them, and left their bodies horribly mutilated. None of the victims was a slaveholder, and two of them were born in Germany and had no contact with the South. By way of explanation Brown said the murders had been "decreed by Almighty God, ordained from Eternity." He later denied responsibility for the act, and some of the Eastern capitalists and intellectuals who supported him refused to believe him guilty. In view of the report of the murders that was laid

before the country on July 11, 1856, in the form of a committee report in the House of Representatives, it is somewhat difficult to excuse such ignorance among intelligent
men.

It was shortly after this report was published, however,
that, for his war on slavery, Brown enjoyed his most striking success in soliciting contributions and making friends
among men of wealth and intellectual distinction in Boston and other Eastern cities. In the first four months of
1858 he succeeded in raising $23,000 in cash, supplies, and
credit to support his guerrilla activities.

In the spring of 1858 plans for a raid on Virginia began
to take definite shape. To a convention of fellow conspirators in Chatham, Canada, in May, John Brown presented his remarkable "Provisional Constitution and Ordi-
nances for the People of the United States." It represented
the form of government he proposed to establish by force
of arms with a handful of conspirators and an armed insurrection of slaves. Complete with legislative, executive,
and judicial branches, Brown's revolutionary government
was in effect a military dictatorship, since all acts of his
congress had to be approved by the commander-in-chief
of the army in order to become valid. Needless to say, John
Brown was elected commander-in-chief.

By July, 1859, Commander-in-Chief Brown had established himself at a farm on the Maryland side of the Potomac River, four miles north of Harpers Ferry. There he
assembled twenty-one followers and accumulated ammuni-
tion and other supplies, including 200 revolvers, 200 rifles,
and 950 pikes specially manufactured for the slaves he

expected to rise up in insurrection. On Sunday night, October 16, after posting a guard of three men at the farm, he set forth with eighteen followers, five of them Negroes, and all of them young men, to start his war of liberation and found his abolitionist republic. Brown's first objective, to capture the United States arsenal at Harpers Ferry, was easily accomplished since it was without military guard. In the Federal armory and the rifle works, also captured, were sufficient arms to start the bloodiest slave insurrection in history.

The commander-in-chief appears to have launched his invasion without any definite plan of campaign and then proceeded to violate every military principle in the book. He cut himself off from his base of supplies, failed to keep open his only avenues of retreat, dispersed his small force, and bottled the bulk of them up in a trap where defeat was inevitable. "In fact, it was so absurd," remarked Abraham Lincoln, "that the slaves, with all their ignorance, saw plainly enough it could not succeed." Not one of them joined Brown voluntarily, and those he impressed quickly departed. The insurrectionists killed one United States Marine and four inhabitants of Harpers Ferry, including the mayor and a Negro freeman. Ten of their own number, including two of Brown's sons, were killed, five were taken prisoner by a small force of Marines commanded by Robert E. Lee, and seven escaped, though two of them were later arrested. John Brown's insurrection ended in a tragic and dismal failure.

When news of the invasion was first flashed across the country, the most common reaction was that this was obviously the act of a madman, that John Brown was insane. This explanation was particularly attractive to Republican politicians and editors, whose party suffered the keenest embarrassment from the incident. Fall elections were on, and the new Congress was about to convene. Democrats immediately charged that John Brown's raid was the inevitable consequence of the "irresistible-conflict" and "higher-law" abolitionism preached by Republican leaders William H. Seward and Salmon P. Chase. "Brown's invasion," wrote Senator Henry Wilson of Massachusetts, "has thrown us, who were in a splendid position, into a defensive position. . . . If we are defeated next year we shall owe it to that foolish and insane movement of Brown's." The emphasis on insanity was taken up widely by Wilson's contemporaries and later adopted by historians.

It seems best to deal with the insanity question promptly, for it is likely to confuse the issue and cause us to miss the meaning of Harpers Ferry. In dealing with the problem it is important not to blink, as many of his biographers have done, at the evidence of John Brown's close association with insanity in both his heredity and his environment. In the Brown Papers at the Library of Congress are nineteen affidavits signed by relatives and friends attesting the record of insanity in the Brown family. John Brown's maternal grandmother and his mother both died insane. His three aunts and two uncles, sisters and brothers of his mother, were intermittently insane, and so was his only sister, her daughter, and one of his brothers. Of six first cousins, all more or less mad, two were deranged from time to time, two had been repeatedly committed to the state insane asylum, and two were still confined at the time. Of John Brown's immediate family, his first wife and one of his sons died insane, and a second son was insane at intervals. On these matters the affidavits, signers of which include Brown's uncle, a half brother, a brother-in-law, and three first cousins, are in substantial agreement. On the sanity of John Brown himself, however, opinion varied. Several believed that he was a "monomaniac," one that he was insane on subjects of religion and slavery, and an uncle thought his nephew had been "subject to periods of insanity" for twenty years.

The insurrectionist himself, of course, stoutly maintained that he was perfectly sane, and he was certainly able to convince many intelligent people, both friend and foe, that he was sane. He firmly refused to plead insanity at his trial. Governor Henry A. Wise of Virginia went so far as to write out orders to the superintendent of the state insane asylum to examine Brown, but endorsed the orders, "countermanded upon reflection." On the other hand, John Brown pronounced Governor Wise mad. "Hard to tell who's mad," jested Wendell Phillips to a laughing congregation in Henry Ward Beecher's church. "The world says one man's mad. John Brown said the same of the Governor. . . . I appeal from Philip drunk to Philip sober." He meant future generations when, he said, "the light of civilization has had more time to penetrate." Then it would be plain that not Brown but his enemies were mad.

We, the Philips sober of the future, with some misgivings about how far "the light of civilization" has penetrated, do think we know a little more about insanity than did our great-grandfathers. We at least know that it is a loose expression for a variety of mental disorders and that it is a relative term. What seems sane to some people at some times seems insane to other people at other times. In our own time we have witnessed what we consider psychopathic personalities rise to power over millions of people and plunge the world into war. Yet to the millions who followed them these leaders appeared sublime in their wisdom.

"John Brown may be a lunatic," observed the Boston *Post,* but if so, "then one-fourth of the people of Massachusetts are madmen," and perhaps three-fourths of the ministers of religion. Begging that Brown's life be spared, Amos A. Lawrence wrote Governor Wise: "Brown is a Puritan whose mind has become disordered by hardship and illness. He has the qualities wh. endear him to our people." The association of ideas was doubtless unintentional, but to the Virginian it must have seemed that Lawrence was saying that in New England a disordered mind was an endearing quality. The Reverend J. M. Manning of Old South Church, Boston, pronounced Harpers Ferry "an unlawful, a foolhardy, a suicidal act" and declared, "I stand before it wondering and admiring." Horace Greeley called it "the work of a madman" for which he had not "one reproachful word," and for the "grandeur and nobility" of which he was "reverently grateful." And the New York *Independent* declared that while "Harpers Ferry was insane, the controlling motive of this demonstration was sublime." It was both foolhardy and godly, insane and sublime, treasonous and admirable.

The prestige and character of the men who lent John Brown active, if sometimes secret, support likewise suggest caution in dismissing Harpers Ferry as merely the work of a madman. Among Brown's fellow conspirators the most notable were the so-called Secret Six. Far from being horse thieves and petty traders, the Secret Six came from the cream of Northern society. Capitalist, philanthropist, philosopher, surgeon, professor, minister—they were men of reputability and learning, four of them with Harvard degrees.

With a Harvard Divinity School degree, a knowledge of twenty languages, and a library of sixteen thousand volumes, Theodore Parker was perhaps the most prodigiously learned American of his time. In constant correspondence with the leading Republican politicians, he has been called "the Conscience of a Party." What Gerrit Smith, the very wealthy philanthropist and one-time congressman of Peterboro, New York, lacked in mental endowments he made up in good works—earnest efforts to improve the habits of his fellow men. These included not only crusades against alcohol and tobacco in all forms, but also coffee, tea, meat, and spices—"almost everything which gave pleasure," according to his biographer. Generous with donations to dietary reform, dress reform, woman's rights, educational and "non-resistance" movements, Smith took no interest whatever in factory and labor reform, but he was passionately absorbed in the antislavery movement and a liberal contributor to John Brown. Dr. Samuel G. Howe of Boston, husband of the famous Julia Ward Howe, was justly renowned for his humanitarian work for the blind and mentally defective. In his youth he had gone on a Byronic crusade in Greece against the Turk. These experiences contributed greatly to his moral prestige, if little to his political sophistication. The most generous man of wealth among the conspirators was George L. Stearns of Boston, a prosperous manufacturer of lead pipe. In the opinion of this revolutionary capitalist, John Brown was "the representative man of this century, as Washington was of the last." Finally there were two younger men, fledgling conspirators. The son of a prosperous Boston merchant who was bursar of Harvard, Thomas Wentworth Higginson became pastor of a church in Worcester after taking his divinity degree at Harvard. Young Franklin B. Sanborn was an apostle of Parker and a protégé of Emerson, who persuaded Sanborn to take charge of a school in Concord.

The most tangible service the Secret Six rendered the conspiracy lay in secretly diverting to John Brown, for use at Harpers Ferry, money and arms that had been contributed to the Massachusetts-Kansas Aid Committee for use in "Bleeding Kansas." This dubious transaction was accomplished by Stearns, chairman of the committee, exercising as a private individual an option he held of foreclosing upon the property of the committee, then promptly transferring the arms to Brown and notifying only the conspirators. By this means the Kansas Committee was converted into a respectable front for subversive purposes, and thousands of innocent contributors to what appeared to be a patriotic organization discovered later that they had furnished rifles for a treasonous attack on a Federal arsenal. Even Sanborn admitted in 1885 that "it is still a little difficult to explain this transaction concerning the arms without leaving the suspicion that there was somewhere a breach of trust." It still is.

The Secret Six appear to have been fascinated by the drama of conspiratorial activity. There were assumed names, coded messages, furtive committee meetings, dissembling of motives, and secret caches of arms. And over all the romance and glamor of a noble cause—the liberation of man. Although they knew perfectly well the general purpose of Brown, the Secret Six were careful to request him not to tell them the precise time and place of the invasion. The wily old revolutionist could have told them much that they did not know about the psychology of fellow travelers. Brown had earlier laid down this strategy for conspirators who were hard pressed: "Go into the houses of your most prominent and influential white friends with your wives; and that will effectually fasten upon them the suspicion of being connected with you, and will compel them to make a common cause with you, whether they would otherwise live up to their professions or not." The same strategy is suggested by Brown's leaving behind, in the Maryland farmhouse where they would inevitably be captured, all his private papers, hundreds of letters of himself and followers, implicating nobody knew how many respectable fellow travelers.

When news of the captured documents arrived, there

occurred a very unheroic panic among the Secret Six, who saw stark ruin and an indictment for treason facing them. Stearns, Sanborn, and Howe fled to Canada. Parker was already abroad. Gerrit Smith's secretary did not stop until he reached England. Smith himself issued pitiable and panicky denials of his guilt, then found refuge in insanity and was confined to an asylum. Howe published a denial unworthy of respect. Higginson alone stood his ground. Stearns and Howe denied any knowledge of the attack before a congressional committee, and both of them told Sanborn they "found the question of the Senate Committee so unskillfully framed that they could, without literal falsehood, answer as they did."

The assistance that the Secret Six conspirators were able to give John Brown and his Legend was as nothing compared with that rendered by other Northern intellectuals. Among them was the cultural and moral aristocracy of America in the period that has been called a "Renaissance." Some of these men, Ralph Waldo Emerson and Henry Thoreau among them, had met and admired Brown and even made small contributions to his cause. But they were safely beyond reproach of the law and were never taken into his confidence in the way that the Secret Six were. Their service was rendered after the event in justifying and glorifying Brown and his invasion.

In this work the intellectuals were ably assisted by a genius, a genius at self-justification—John Brown himself. From his prison cell he poured out a stream of letters, serene and restrained, filled with Biblical language and fired with overpowering conviction that his will and God's were one and the same. These letters and his famous speech at the trial constructed for the hero a new set of motives and plans and a new role. For Brown had changed roles. In October he invaded Virginia as a conqueror armed for conquest, carrying with him guns and pikes for the army he expected to rally to his standard and a new constitution to replace the one he overthrew. In that role he was a miserable failure. Then in November he declared at his trial: "I never did intend murder, or treason, or the destruction of property, or to excite or incite slaves to rebellion, or to make an insurrection." He only intended to liberate slaves without bloodshed, as he falsely declared he had done in Missouri the year before. How these statements can be reconciled with the hundreds of pikes, revolvers, and rifles, the capture of an armory, the taking of hostages, the killing of unarmed civilians, the destruction of government property, and the arming of slaves is difficult to see. Nor is it possible to believe that Brown thought he could seize a Federal arsenal, shoot down United States Marines, and overthrow a government without committing treason. "It was all so thin," as Robert Penn Warren has observed of the trial speech, "that it should not have deceived a child, but it deceived a generation." At Lincoln's funeral Emerson compared it with the Gettysburg Address.

Emerson seemed hesitant in his first private reactions to Harpers Ferry. Thoreau, on the other hand, never hesitated a moment. On the day after Brown's capture he compared the hero's inevitable execution with the crucifixion of Christ. Harpers Ferry was "the best news that America ever had"; Brown, "the bravest and humanest man in all the country," "a Transcendentalist above all," and he declared: "I rejoice that I live in this age, that I was his contemporary." Emerson quickly fell into line with Thoreau, and in his November 8 lecture on "Courage" described Brown as "the saint, whose fate yet hangs in suspense, but whose martyrdom, if it shall be perfected, will make the gallows as glorious as the cross." Within a few weeks Emerson gave three important lectures, in all of which he glorified John Brown.

With the Sage of Concord and his major prophet in accord on the martyr, the majority of the transcendental hierarchy sooner or later joined in—William E. Channing, Bronson and Louisa May Alcott, Longfellow, Bryant, and Lowell, and of course Wendell Phillips and Theodore Parker. Parker pronounced Brown "not only a martyr . . . but also a SAINT." Thoreau and Henry Ward Beecher frankly admitted they hoped Brown would hang. To spare a life would be to spoil a martyr. They were interested in him not as a man but as a symbol, a moral ideal, and a saint for a crusade. In the rituals of canonization the gallows replaced the cross as a symbol. Louisa May Alcott called the gallows "a stepping-stone to heaven"; Parker, "the road to heaven"; Theodore Tilton, "a throne greater than a king's"; and Phillips concluded that "henceforth it is sacred forever."

Among Western antislavery men there were fewer intellectuals of fame or notoriety, but abolitionist preachers, teachers, and orators joined in apotheosizing Brown. Citizens of Oberlin erected a monument to three Negroes who gave their lives in Brown's raid. And Theodore D.

Weld, once the genius of Western abolitionism, though in retirement, permitted burial of two of the Harpers Ferry raiders at his school in New Jersey. Not all of the Northern intellectuals became members of the Brown cult. Nathaniel Hawthorne and Walt Whitman were two notable dissenters. Devotees of the cult showed little tolerance for dissent. Emerson declared that "all people, in proportion to their sensibility and self-respect, sympathize with him [Brown]," and Thoreau carried intolerance to the point of moral snobbery. "When a noble deed is done, who is likely to appreciate it? They who are noble themselves," answered Thoreau. "I was not surprised that certain of my neighbors spoke of John Brown as an ordinary felon, for who are they? They have either much flesh, or much office, or much coarseness of some kind. They are not ethereal natures in any sense. The dark qualities predominate in them. . . . For the children of the light to contend with them is as if there should be a contest between eagles and owls."

The task to which the intellectuals of the cult dedicated themselves was the idealizing of John Brown as a symbol of the moral order and the social purpose of the Northern cause. Wendell Phillips expressed this best when he declared in the Boston Music Hall: " 'Law' and 'order' are only means for the halting ignorance of the last generation. John Brown is the impersonation of God's order and God's law, moulding a better future, and setting for it an example." In substituting the new revolutionary law and order for traditional law and order, the intellectuals encountered some tough problems in morals and values. It was essential for them to justify a code of political methods and morals that was at odds with the Anglo-American tradition.

John Brown's own solution to this problem was quite simple. It is set forth in the preamble of his Provisional Constitution of the United States, which declares that in reality slavery is an "unjustifiable War of one portion of its citizens upon another." War, in which all is fair, amounted to a suspension of ethical restraints. This type of reasoning is identical with that of the revolutionaries who hold that class struggle is in reality a class war. The assumption naturally facilitates the justification of deeds otherwise indefensible. These might include the dissembling of motives, systematic deception, theft, murder, or the liquidation of an enemy class.

It is clear that certain enthusiasts found in Brown's reasoning a satisfactory solution to their moral problem, but it was equally clear that the mass of people were not yet ready to accept this solution and that some other rationalization was required. The doctrine of the "Higher Law" and the doctrine of "Civil Disobedience" had already done much to prepare the way for acceptance of the revolutionary ethics. They had justified conduct in defiance of the Constitution and the government by appeal to higher moral ends. Transcendental doctrine was now used to extend the defiance of tradition even further. Thoreau's reply to attacks upon John Brown's methods was: "The method is nothing; the spirit is all." This was the Transcendentalist way of saying that means are justified by the ends. According to this doctrine, if the end is sufficiently noble—as noble as the emancipation of the slave—any means used to attain the end is justified.

The crisis of Harpers Ferry was a crisis of means, not of ends. John Brown did not raise the question of whether slavery should be abolished or tolerated. That question had been raised in scores of ways and debated for a generation. Millions held strong convictions on the subject. Upon abolition, as an *end,* there was no difference between John Brown and the American and Foreign Anti-Slavery Society. But as to the *means* of attaining abolition, there was as much difference between them, so far as the record goes, as there is between the modern British Labour Party and the government of Soviet Russia on the means of abolishing capitalism. The Anti-Slavery Society was solemnly committed to the position of nonviolent means. In the very petition that Lewis Tappan, secretary of the society, addressed to Governor Wise in behalf of Brown he repeated the rubric about "the use of all carnal weapons for deliverance from bondage." But in their rapture over Brown as martyr and saint the abolitionists lost sight of their differences with him over the point of means and ended by totally compromising their creed of nonviolence.

But what of those who clung to the democratic principle that differences should be settled by ballots and that the will of the majority should prevail? Phillips pointed out: "In God's world there are no majorities, no minorities; one, on God's side, is a majority." And Thoreau asked, "When were the good and the brave ever in a majority?" So much for majority rule. What of the issue of treason?

The Reverend Fales H. Newhall of Roxbury declared that the word "treason" had been "made holy in the American language"; and the Reverend Edwin M. Wheelock of Boston blessed "the sacred, and the radiant 'treason' of John Brown."

No aversion to bloodshed seemed to impede the spread of the Brown cult. William Lloyd Garrison thought that "every slaveholder has forfeited his right to live" if he impeded emancipation. The Reverend Theodore Parker predicted a slave insurrection in which "The Fire of Vengeance" would run "from man to man, from town to town" through the South. "What shall put it out?" he asked. "The White Man's blood." The Reverend Mr. Wheelock thought Brown's "mission was to inaugurate slave insurrection as the divine weapon of the antislavery cause." He asked: "Do we shrink from the bloodshed that would follow?" and answered, "No such wrong [as slavery] was ever cleansed by rose-water." Rather than see slavery continued the Reverend George B. Cheever of New York declared: "It were infinitely better that three hundred thousand slaveholders were abolished, struck out of existence." In these pronouncements the doctrine that the end justifies the means had arrived pretty close to justifying the liquidation of an enemy class.

The reactions of the extremists have been stressed in part because it was the extremist view that eventually prevailed in the apotheosis of John Brown and, in part, because by this stage of the crisis each section tended to judge the other by the excesses of a few. "Republicans were all John Browns to the Southerners," as Professor Dwight

L. Dumond has observed, "and slaveholders were all Simon Legrees to the Northerners." As a matter of fact Northern conservatives and unionists staged huge anti-Brown demonstrations that equaled or outdid those staged by the Brown partisans. Nathan Appleton wrote a Virginian: "I have never in my long life seen a fuller or more enthusiastic demonstration" than the anti-Brown meeting in Faneuil Hall in Boston. The Republican press described a similar meeting in New York as "the largest and most enthusiastic" ever held in that city. Northern politicians of high rank, including Lincoln, Douglas, Seward, Edward Everett, and Henry Wilson, spoke out against John Brown and his methods. The Republican party registered its official position by a plank in the 1860 platform denouncing the Harpers Ferry raid. Lincoln approved of Brown's execution, "even though he agreed with us in thinking slavery wrong." Agreement on ends did not mean agreement on means. "That cannot excuse violence, bloodshed, and treason," said Lincoln.

Republican papers of the Western states as well as of the East took pains to dissociate themselves from Harpers Ferry, and several denounced the raid roundly. At first conservative Southern papers, for example the *Arkansas State Gazette,* rejoiced that "the leading papers, and men, among the Black Republicans, are open . . . in their condemnation of the course of Brown." As the canonization of Brown advanced, however, the Republican papers gradually began to draw a distinction between their condemnation of Brown's raid and their high regard for the man himself—his courage, his integrity, and his noble motives.

They also tended to find, in the wrongs Brown and his men had suffered at the hands of slaveholders in Kansas, much justification for his attack upon Virginia. From that it was an easy step to pronounce the raid a just retribution for the South's violence in Kansas. There was enough ambiguity about Republican disavowal of Brown to leave doubts in many minds. If Lincoln deplored Brown, Lincoln's partner Billy Herndon worshipped Brown. If there was one editor who condemned the raid, there were a half dozen who admired its leader. To Southerners the distinction was elusive or entirely unimportant.

Northern businessmen were foremost in deprecating Harpers Ferry and reassuring the South. Some of them linked their denunciation of Brown with a defense of slavery, however, so that in the logic that usually prevails in time of crisis all critics of Brown risked being smeared with the charge of defending slavery. Radicals called them mossbacks, doughfaces, appeasers, and sought to jeer them out of countenance. "If they cannot be converted, [they] may yet be scared," was Parker's doctrine.

Among the Brown partisans not one has been found but who believed that Harpers Ferry had resulted in great gain for the extremist cause. So profoundly were they convinced of this that they worried little over the conservative dissent. "How vast the change in men's hearts!" exclaimed Phillips. "Insurrection was a harsh, horrid word to millions a month ago." Now it was "the lesson of the hour." Garrison rejoiced that thousands who could not listen to his gentlest rebuke ten years before "now easily

swallow John Brown whole, and his rifle in the bargain."
"They all called him crazy then," wrote Thoreau; "Who
calls him crazy now?" To the poet it seemed that "the
North is suddenly all Transcendentalist." On the day John
Brown was hanged church bells were tolled in com-
memoration in New England towns, out along the Mo-
hawk Valley, in Cleveland and the Western Reserve, in
Chicago and northern Illinois. In Albany one hundred
rounds were fired from a cannon. Writing to his daughter
the following day, Joshua Giddings of Ohio said, "I find
the hatred of slavery greatly intensified by the fate of
Brown and men are ready to march to Virginia and dispose of her despotism at once." It was not long before they
were marching to Virginia, and marching to the tune of
"John Brown's Body."

The Harpers Ferry crisis on the other side of the Potomac was a faithful reflection of the crisis in the North,
and can therefore be quickly sketched. It is the reflection,
with the image reversed in the mirror, that antagonistic
powers present to each other in a war crisis. To the South
John Brown also appeared as a true symbol of Northern
purpose, but instead of the "angel of light" Thoreau pictured, the South saw an angel of destruction. The South
did not seriously question Brown's sanity either, for he
seemed only the rational embodiment of purposes that
Southern extremists had long taught were universal in
the North. The crisis helped propagandists falsely identify
the whole North with John Brownism. For Harpers Ferry

strengthened the hand of extremists and revolutionists in the South as it did in the North, and it likewise discredited and weakened moderates and their influence.

The risk one runs in describing the reaction to Harpers Ferry is the risk of attributing to that event tendencies long manifest. The South had been living in a crisis atmosphere for a long time. It was a society in the grip of an insecurity complex, a tension resulting from both rational and irrational fears. One cause of it was the steady, invincible expansion of the free-state system in size and power, after the Southern system had reached the limits of its own expansion. The South, therefore, felt itself to be menaced through encirclement by a power containing elements unfriendly to its interests, elements that were growing strong enough to capture the government. The South's insecurity was heightened by having to defend against constant attack an institution it knew to be discredited throughout the civilized world and of which Southerners had once been among the severest critics. Its reaction was to withdraw increasingly from contact with the offending world, to retreat into an isolationism of spirit, and to attempt by curtailing freedom of speech to avoid criticism.

One of the South's tensions sprang from a lack of internal security—the fear of servile insurrection. By the nature of things a slave uprising had to be secret, sudden, and extremely bloody, sparing neither men, women, nor children. The few occurrences of this kind had left a deep trauma in the minds of the people. The pathological character of this tension was manifested in periodic waves of panic based largely on rumor. It is significant that two of the most severe panics of this sort occurred in the election years 1856 and 1860 and were accompanied by charges that abolitionists from the North were fomenting uprisings. Harpers Ferry was therefore a blow at the most sensitive area of Southern consciousness.

The first reaction to the raid, outside Virginia, was surprisingly mild. Newspapers, particularly in the Lower South, pointed out that, after all, the slaves had remained loyal, that Brown's invasion was a complete failure, and that it was quickly suppressed. This mood did not last long, however. The hundreds of captured documents belonging to Brown and his men persuaded Virginia authorities that the conspiracy was widespread and that the Harpers Ferry strike, had it been successful, was intended to be merely the signal for uprisings throughout the South. Among the documents were maps of seven Southern states with certain widely scattered areas and localities marked with symbols. The symbols may have indicated nothing at all, of course, but they were enough to grip the localities concerned with fear.

Another document that inspired terror was a long letter from Lawrence Thatcher (an assumed name), one of Brown's emissaries, reporting two weeks before the raid on a tour of the South. Written from Memphis, the letter suggests the presence of a formidable force of subversives established in the South by Brown's organization. In Tennessee and Arkansas there were reported to be "an immense number of slaves ripe and ready at the very first intimation to strike a decided blow," and the writer was amazed to find "so large a number of whites ready to aid us" in Memphis. A "thorough scouring" of Arkansas convinced him that the readiness of the slaves was such that "a bold stroke of one day will overthrow the whole state." In Brownsville, Tennessee, a subversive white schoolteacher urged that "we must send out more well qualified men to the South as school teachers, and work them in everywhere," that there was "no avocation in which a man can do so much good for our cause" since the people had so much confidence in a schoolteacher. The writer of the letter assured John Brown that "Southern people are easy gulled." His report reveals the man as a wishful thinker and a naïve enthusiast, but after Harpers Ferry, when this letter was found by Virginia authorities, the Southern mind was in no state to distinguish between responsible and irresponsible sources of evidence.

Letters from all parts of the South deluged Governor Wise's mail with reports that Brown conspirators had been seized or punished. These, and the Southern newspapers of the time, portray a society in the throes of panic. Convinced that the South was honeycombed with subversives, Southerners tended to see an abolitionist behind every bush and a slave insurrection brewing in the arrival of any stranger. Victims of vigilante and mob action ranged from aged eccentrics and itinerant piano-tuners to substantial citizens of long residence. The mob spirit was no respecter of person or class. A sixty-year-old minister in Texas, who was a believer in the Biblical sanction of slavery and a Democrat of Kentucky birth, made the mistake of criticizing the treatment of slaves in a sermon and was given seventy lashes on his back. A schoolteacher who had lived in Louisiana and Arkansas for ten years was given thirty-six hours to leave the latter state. The newly arrived president of an Alabama college, who came from New York, was forced to give up his job and flee for his life. In December, 1859, twelve families, including thirty-nine people associated with antislavery schools and churches of Berea, Kentucky, were forcibly expelled from the state for abolitionism.

Southern fire-eaters swore that no Northerner could be trusted and that all should be expelled. Even the humblest workmen from the North were in danger of insult, violence, or lynching. An Irish stonecutter in Columbia, South Carolina, was beaten, tarred and feathered, and expelled from the state by a mob. Three members of the crew of a brig from Maine were brutally flogged in Georgia, and a New England mechanic was driven out of a village in the same state because he was found to have a clean shirt wrapped in a New York paper containing one of Beecher's sermons. Two Connecticut book-peddlers were roughly handled in Charleston when lists of slaves were found in their bags, and two printers were ridden out of Kingstree, South Carolina, on rails. Four men "suspected of being abolition emissaries" were arrested in two days in Columbus, Georgia, and ten peddlers were driven out of the village of Abbeville, Mississippi. Four months after Harpers Ferry a man was lynched in South Carolina as "one of Brown's associates." Not only Northerners but associates of Northerners were subject to persecution, for guilt by association was an accepted principle in the crisis.

Then there was the Southern enemy within the gates to be dealt with. Hinton R. Helper of North Carolina had written an antislavery book, quantities of which were burned in public ceremonies at High Point in his own state, at Greenville, South Carolina, and at Mayesville, Kentucky. Other public book-burning ceremonies took place at Enterprise, Mississippi, and at Montgomery, Alabama, while at Palestine, Texas, the citizens appointed a committee "to collect all said dangerous books for destruction by public burning." Thought control extended to the suppression and seizure of newspapers, a method long practiced, and in Alabama a resolution was introduced in the legislature prohibiting the licensing of teachers with less than ten years' residence, "to protect the state against abolition teachers." Not content with cutting off intellectual commerce with the North, extremists organized to end economic intercourse as well. They published blacklists of Northern firms suspected of abolitionist tendencies, organized boycotts, and promoted nonintercourse agreements. The Richmond *Enquirer* advocated a law "that will keep out of our borders every article of Northern manufacture or importation." On December 8, 1859, thirty-two business agents of New York and Boston arrived in Washington from the South, reporting "indignation so great against Northerners that they were compelled to return and abandon their business."

Southern zealots of secession had no better ally than John Brown. Robert B. Rhett, Edmund Ruffin, and William L. Yancey all rejoiced over the effect of Harpers Ferry. Nonslaveholders saw dramatized before them the menace of a slave uprising and readily concluded that their wives and children, as much as the home of the planter, were threatened with the horror of insurrection. They frequently became more fanatical secessionists than the planters. In face of the Northern apotheosis of Brown there was little that Southern moderates could say in answer to such pronouncements as that of the New Orleans *Picayune* of December 2: "Crime becomes godliness, and criminals, red from the slaughter of innocent, are exalted to eminence beside the divine gospel of Peace." The Charleston *Mercury* of November 29 rejoiced that Harpers Ferry, "like a slap in the face," had roused Virginia from her hesitant neutrality and started her on the road to secession. "I have never before seen the public mind of Va. so deeply moved," wrote a Virginian sadly. "The people are far in advance of the politicians, and would most cheerfully follow the extremist counsels. Volunteer companies, horse & foot, are springing up everywhere."

The crisis psychology of 1859 persisted and deepened in the fateful year of 1860 into a pathological condition of mind in which delusions of persecution and impending disaster flourished. Out of Texas came wild rumors of incendiary fires, abolitionists plotting with slaves, and impending insurrection on a vast scale. Rumors of large stocks of strychnine in the possession of slaves and of plans for well-poisoning were widely believed, though unproved. One scholar has aptly compared the tension of the South in 1860 with the "Great Fear" that seized the rural provinces of France in the summer of 1789 when panic spread the word that "the brigands are coming." In that atmosphere the South made the momentous decision that split the Democratic Party at Charleston in April, and before the mood was gone it was debating secession.

In the course of the crisis each of the antagonists, according to the immemorial pattern, had become convinced of the depravity and diabolism of the other. Each believed itself persecuted, menaced. "Let the 'higher law' of abolitionism be met by the 'higher law' of self-preservation," demanded the Richmond *Enquirer*. Lynch law was the only answer to pikes. "What additional insults and outrages *will* arouse it [the North] to assert its rights?" demanded Garrison. And Garrison's opposite number in Mississippi, Albert Gallatin Brown, cried: "Oh, God! To what depths of infamy are we sinking in the South if we allow these things to pass." Paranoia continued to induce counterparanoia, each antagonist infecting the other reciprocally, until the vicious spiral ended in war.

4

Equality: The Deferred Commitment

Now THAT THE DRIVE IS ON TO GIVE ACCUSTOMED CANT
about equality for the Negro some basis in fact and to
deliver on promises nearly a century old, the temptation
is strong to pretend that we have been in earnest all along.
Such a pretense, successfully maintained, might stiffen
resolution, put the forces of resistance further on the defensive, and in general further a good cause. Before we
become so deeply committed to the pretense that we believe in it ourselves, however, it would be well to look
soberly into the curious origins of the commitment to
equality during the Civil War and into its subsequent
abandonment.

The North had a much more difficult time defining its
war aims than the South. The aims of the South were fixed
and obvious from the start and remained constant until
rendered hopeless—the establishment and defense of independence. The North moved gradually and gropingly
toward a definition of its war aims. Its progress was ob-
structed by doubt and misgiving and characterized by

much backing and filling. The debate and the outcome were shaped by the course of the war itself, by military necessities, foreign propaganda needs, and domestic morale demands, as well as by the exigencies of party politics and political ambitions.

As the North progressed toward the framing of war objectives, America was inched along from right to left. It moved from hesitant support of a limited war with essentially negative aims toward a total war with positive and revolutionary aims. The character of the war changed from a pragmatic struggle for power to a crusade for ideals. The struggle took on many aspects of an ideological war, and in some minds became a holy war, fought, financed, and supported by men who could feel themselves instruments of divine will.

It was far different at the outset. Lincoln was inaugurated President of a slaveholding republic. He had been elected on a platform firmly pledging him to the protection of the institution of slavery where it existed, and in his first inaugural address, while not abandoning his moral views of slavery, he explicitly denied that he entertained any "purpose, directly or indirectly, to interfere with the institution of slavery in the states where it exists." Not only had he no purpose, but he declared he had "no lawful right" and indeed, "no inclination to do so." He assured the people of the South that their property was not "in any wise endangered by the now incoming administration." His emphasis was upon the negative aim of preventing secession and the disruption of the Union.

Four and a half months later, after blood had been shed

and the war was in full swing, Congress took a hand in defining war aims. On July 22 the House adopted, with only two negative votes, a resolution declaring that "this war is not waged . . . [for the] purpose of overthrowing or interfering with the . . . established institutions of those States, but to . . . maintain . . . the . . . States unimpaired; and that as soon as these objects are accomplished the war ought to cease." The Senate backed this sentiment up with a similar resolution, also adopted by a nearly unanimous vote. At this stage, so far as both President and Congress were able to formulate war aims, this was a war of narrowly limited objectives and no revolutionary purpose. It was to be a war against secession, a war to maintain the Union—that, and nothing more.

This negative phase did not last long. No mood lasted very long in the flux and change of the Civil War. Five months later the House voted down a motion to reaffirm the resolution of limited war aims. Already the movement was under way to extend those aims from mere Union to embrace freedom as well. The second war aim was not attained by a stroke of Lincoln's pen, as Lincoln was the first to admit. It was forced by events, by necessities, and those events and necessities first took the shape of thousands of pitiable fugitive slaves crowding into the Union lines. Their path toward freedom was tedious and rugged, filled with obstacles. Thousands wavered between freedom and slavery for years and were never quite sure when freedom came, or if it did. The majority only began their struggle for freedom after the war was over.

Freedom as a war aim was arrived at by a long succession of piecemeal decisions. There were orders by field commanders, some countermanded, some sustained; there were acts of state legislatures; and there was a long succession of bits and driblets of emancipation enacted by Congress, which did not get around to repealing the Fugitive Slave Act until June of 1864. And always there was the embarrassed and reluctant dragon of emancipation, the invading army. "Although war has not been waged against slavery," wrote Secretary Seward to Charles Francis Adams in 1862, "yet the army acts . . . as an emancipating crusade. To proclaim the crusade is unnecessary."

The crusade *was* eventually proclaimed, though the proclamation was not the President's. Lincoln never wanted to turn the war into a moral crusade. It is not necessary to retrace here the painful steps by which Lincoln arrived at his numerous decisions upon slavery and emancipation. It is sometimes forgotten, however, how often he deprecated the importance of his Proclamation of Emancipation. He characterized it as a war necessity, forced by events, ineffectual, inadequate, and of doubtful legality. It is plain that his heart was in his plan for gradual emancipation, which he repeatedly but unsuccessfully urged upon Congress and proposed as a Constitutional amendment. This was an extremely conservative plan for gradual and voluntary emancipation over a period of thirty-seven years, to be completed by 1900, to be administered by the slave states themselves, and to be assisted by the Federal government with compensation to slaveowners and foreign colonization of freedmen. Support was not forthcoming, and war developments underlined the impracticality of the plan.

When Lincoln finally resorted to the Proclamation, he presented it as a war measure, authorized by war powers and justified by military necessity. Again and again he repeated that it was a means to an end—the limited Lincolnian end of union—and not an end in itself, that union and not freedom was the true war aim. Yet freedom had become a second war aim anyway, and for many the primary war aim. In spite of the fact that the Proclamation emancipated no slaves, it had a profound effect upon the war—more effect upon the war, in fact, than upon slavery.

For one thing, it helped to elevate the war to a new plane. It was still a war for union, but not as before—a war for union with slavery. It was no longer merely a war against something, but a war for something, a war for something greatly cherished in American tradition and creed, a war for freedom. What had started as a war for political ends had, by virtue of military necessity, undergone a metamorphosis into a higher and finer thing, a war for moral ends. What had commenced as a police action had been converted into a crusade. Some abolitionists professed disappointment in the Proclamation, but so ardent a believer as Theodore Tilton was in "a bewilderment of joy" with the new spirit "so racing up and down and through my blood that I am half crazy with enthusiasm."

The great majority of citizens in the North still abhorred any association with abolitionists, but any of them were now free to share the forbidden transports of the despised radicals at no cost to their reputation whatever. Conservative, humdrum, unheroic millions could now sing "John Brown's Body" in naïve identification with the demented old hero and partake, vicariously and quite inexpensively, of his martyrdom. An aura of glory descended upon the common cause that sometimes lifted men out of themselves, exalted them, though it seems to have inspired civilians and noncombatants more often than soldiers. It could endow men with a sense of moral superiority and divine purpose that enabled them to regard the enemy with a new indignation and righteousness. It emboldened them to make messianic pronouncements with no apparent self-consciousness. The exuberant religiosity of the age was tapped for war propaganda and yielded riches. How otherwise could men, with no consciousness of blasphemy, lift their voices to sing, "As He died to make men holy, let us die to make men free"?

Before he issued the proclamation, Lincoln had written privately that he was holding the antislavery pressure "within bounds." He could no longer make that boast with assurance, for after the edict of January 1, 1863, antislavery sentiment could not always be kept in bounds. As Professor James G. Randall put it, "The concomitants of emancipation got out of Lincoln's hands. He could issue his proclamation, but he could not control the radicals." The "concomitant" of the second war aim of freedom was a third—equality. No sooner was the Union officially committed to the second war aim than the drive was on for commitment to the third.

It cannot be said that this drive was as successful as the

movement for freedom, nor that by the end of the war the country was committed to equality in the same degree it was to freedom. There was no Equality Proclamation to match the Emancipation Proclamation. The third war aim never gained from Lincoln even the qualified support he gave to abolition. Without presidential blessing the commitment was eventually made, made piecemeal like that to freedom, and with full implications not spelled out until after the war—but it was made.

The formal commitment to the third war aim would never have been possible had the abolitionist minority not been able to appeal to more venerable and acceptable doctrine than their own. It would be preposterous to credit the abolitionists with surreptitiously introducing the idea of equality into America. The nation was born with the word on its tongue. The first of those "self-evident" truths of the Declaration was that "all men are created equal." Back of that was the heritage of natural rights doctrine, and back of that the great body of Christian dogma and the teaching that all men are equal in the sight of God.

There were, of course, less disinterested inducements in operation. If freedom was in part a military expedient, equality was in part a political and economic expedient. Equality of the franchise for freedmen was deemed essential to Republican supremacy, and Republican supremacy was considered necessary by influential classes to protect the new economic order.

Equality was advisable, not only politically and economically, but also from a psychological and religious standpoint. For fulfillment of abolitionist purposes it was almost a necessity. Abolitionists had grounded their whole crusade against slavery on the proposition that it was a "sin." It is not sufficient simply to abolish a sin; it has to be expiated, and the sinner purified. Purification and expiation involve penance and suffering. Equality had a punitive purpose: the infliction of a penance of humiliation upon the status of the sinner. For those with an uncomplicated interest in sheer vengeance upon a hated foe, equality had punitive uses of a simpler sort.

Even with all these resources at their command, however, the radicals could never have succeeded in their drive for the formal commitment to equality had it not been launched upon the mounting tide of war spirit and had the war not already been converted into a moral crusade. A moral crusade could only be justified by high moral aims, even if those aims were embraced by the great majority as an afterthought, by many with important mental reservations, and by others as expedients for extraneous ends having nothing whatever to do with the welfare of the freedmen.

So far as the abolitionist minority was concerned, the association of freedom and equality, as Jacobus tenBroek has demonstrated, was rooted in three decades of organized antislavery agitation. Antislavery congressmen carried this association of aims into the framing of the Thirteenth Amendment. Debates over the question in the Senate in the spring of 1864 and in the House of Representatives in January, 1865, contain evidence that the framers aimed at equality as well as emancipation. Both objectives were assumed by the opponents as well as the sponsors of the amendment during the debate. As one of the supporters, William D. Kelley of Pennsylvania, put it: "The proposed Amendment is designed . . . to accomplish . . . the abolition of slavery in the United States, and the political and social elevation of Negroes to all the rights of white men." His broad construction of the amendment was echoed with variations by numerous supporters. They did not include enfranchisement among the rights of Negroes, but they specifically and repeatedly mentioned equal protection of the laws, safeguard for privileges and immunities, and guarantee against deprivation of life, liberty, and property without due process of law. The main ground of opposition to the amendment was this very aim of equality. A constant complaint of opponents was that the amendment would not only free the Negroes but would "make them our equals before the law."

The broad construction of the Thirteenth Amendment to include equality as well as freedom was not sustained when put to test, and the radicals themselves abandoned the interpretation. But they did not abandon their aim of equality. Instead, they increased the scope of it. Responding to provocation of Southern aggression against Negro rights and to inducement of political gains as well, they proceeded to make equality as much the law of the land as freedom. In the Civil Rights Act of 1866 they gave sweeping protection to the rights of Negroes as citizens, guaranteeing them "full and equal benefit of all laws and proceedings for security of person and property, as is enjoyed by white citizens," regardless of any law to the contrary. When the President vetoed the bill, they passed it over his veto. When doubt was cast upon its constitutionality, they enacted most of its provisions into the Fourteenth Amendment. When the South balked at ratification, they stipulated its adoption as a condition of readmission to the Union. Later they extended Federal protection to the Negro franchise by the Fifteenth Amendment. They re-enacted the Civil Rights Act, implementing protection of voters, and followed that by another bill to carry out rights established by the Fourteenth Amendment. To crown the achievement they passed still another Civil Rights Act in 1875 which provided sweepingly that "all persons within the jurisdiction of the United States shall be entitled to the full and equal enjoyment of the accommodations, advantages, facilities, and privileges of inns, public conveyances on land or water, theatres, and other places of public amusement, subject only to the conditions and limitations established by law and applicable alike to citizens of every race and color, regardless of any previous condition of servitude."

Thus, by every device of emphasis, repetition, re-enactment, and reiteration, the radical lawmakers and Constitution-amenders would seem to have nailed down all loose ends, banished all ambiguity, and left no doubt whatever about their intention to extend Federal protection to Negro equality. So far as it was humanly possible to do so by statute and constitutional amendment, America would seem to have been firmly committed to the principle of equality.

And yet we know that within a very short time after

these imposing commitments were made they were broken. America reneged, shrugged off the obligation, and all but forgot about it for nearly a century. The commitments to the war aims of union and freedom were duly honored, but not the third commitment. In view of current concern over the default and belated effort to make amends, it might be of interest to inquire how and why it ever occurred.

Equality was a far more revolutionary aim than freedom, though it may not have seemed so at first. Slavery seemed so formidable, so powerfully entrenched in law and property, and so fiercely defended by arms that it appeared far the greater obstacle. Yet slavery was property based on law. The law could be changed and the property expropriated. Not so inequality. Its entrenchments were deeper and subtler. The attainment of equality involved many more relationships than those between master and slave. It was a revolution that was not confined to the boundaries of the defeated and discredited South, as emancipation largely was. It was a revolution for the North as well. It involved such unpredictable and biased people as hotel clerks, railroad conductors, steamboat stewards, theater ushers, real estate agents, and policemen. In fact, it could involve almost anybody. It was clear from the start that this revolution was going to require enthusiastic and widespread support in the North to make it work.

Was there any such support? Who were the American people so firmly committed to this revolutionary change, and what degree of support were they prepared to lend it? For one thing, among the Union-supporting people were those of the border area, which included not only Kentucky, Missouri, and West Virginia but also the Southern parts of Ohio, Indiana, and Illinois. This area embraced a white population approximately equal to the number of whites in the Confederate states. And if Maryland be added, as I think it should be, that area included considerably more white people than the Confederacy. Most of those people were still living in slave states during the war, and many of their attitudes and habits were not very different from those of people in states to the southward. Their enthusiasm for the third war aim was a matter of some doubt.

What of the Republican party itself, the party responsible for enacting the commitment to equality? During the war it was, of course, exclusively a sectional party, a party of Northern people. Its membership was heavily recruited from the defunct Whig party, and the new party never shook off its Whiggish origins. Many of its members, to use Lincoln's phrase, disliked being "unwhigged." The essence of Whiggery was accommodation and compromise, compromise of many kinds, including the old type of sectional compromise. Before Reconstruction was over, Republicans were again seeking out their old Whig friends of the South with proffered compromise that would leave the solution of the race question in Southern hands.

Lincoln was fully aware of the limited moral resources of his party and his section of the country. He knew that there were limits beyond which popular conviction and conscience could not be pushed in his time. Whatever his personal convictions—and he may, as one historian has maintained, have been entirely color blind—when he spoke as President of the United States or as leader of his political party, he spoke with measured words. And he did not speak in one way to Negroes and another to whites. To a delegation of Negro leaders at the White House he said, "There is an unwillingness on the part of our people, harsh as it may be, for you free colored people to remain with us." He expressed deep sympathy for their wrongs as slaves. "But even when you cease to be slaves," he said, "you are yet far removed from being placed on an equality with the white race. . . . The aspiration of men is to enjoy equality with the best when free, but on this broad continent not a single man of your race is made the equal of a single man of ours. . . . I cannot alter it if I would. It is a fact. . . . It is better for us both, therefore, to be separated." This idea of separating the races led Lincoln to support the most impractical and illusory plan of his entire career, the plan for colonizing the freedmen abroad or settling them in segregated colonies at home.

What were the sentiments of the Federal Army—the army of liberation—about the issue of equality? That great body included eventually more than two million men. There appears to have been a lower proportion of men from the upper income and social classes, and a higher proportion of the lower economic and social order in the Federal than in the Confederate Army. But there were men of all kinds and all views. Among them were officers and enlisted men of deep and abiding conviction, dedi-

cated spirits whose devotion to the moral aims of the war
is borne out in their conduct and in their treatment of
slaves, freedmen, and Negro soldiers.

Unfortunately it cannot be said that soldiers of this turn
of mind were typical of the army sentiment, or even that
they were very numerous. They seem, on the contrary, to
have been quite untypical. "One who reads letters and
diaries of Union soldiers," writes Professor Bell I. Wiley,
who has indeed read many of them, "encounters an enor-
mous amount of antipathy toward Negroes. Expressions
of unfriendliness range from blunt statements bespeaking
intense hatred to belittling remarks concerning dress and
demeanor." Many of the Union soldiers brought their race
prejudices with them from civilian life. Sometimes these
prejudices were mitigated by contact with the Negro, but
more often they appear to have been intensified and augmented by army experience. Men who endure the hard-
ships and suffering and boredom of war have always
sought scapegoats on which to heap their miseries. In the
Civil War the Negroes who crowded into Union lines
were made to order for the role of scapegoat. The treatment they often received at the hands of their liberators
makes some of the darkest pages of war history. Another
shameful chapter is the treatment of the 200,000 Negroes
who served in the Union Army. Enlistment of Negroes
in the first place appears to have been strongly opposed
by the great majority of white troops. And even after their
battle record proved, as Dudley T. Cornish says, "that
Negro soldiers measured up to the standard set for American soldiers generally," they continued to be discriminated

against by unequal pay, allowances, and opportunities. These inequalities lasted throughout the war. It would seem at times that the army of liberation marched southward on its crusade under the banner of White Supremacy.

One is driven by the evidence to the conclusion that the radicals committed the country to a guarantee of equality that popular convictions were not prepared to sustain, that legal commitments overreached moral persuasion. The lag between conviction and commitment could be illustrated by many more examples, including race riots and violent labor demonstrations against the Negro that broke out during the war in Cleveland, Cincinnati, Chicago, Detroit, Buffalo, Albany, Brooklyn and New York. The tendency would also be revealed by the neglect, exclusion, or hostility that craft unions and national unions exhibited toward the Negro during the war years and afterward. Further illustration could be drawn from the measures adopted by Western states to discourage freedmen from settling or working within their boundaries, or going to school with their children. One should also recall that in all but a handful of Northern states suffrage was denied the Negro long after it was mandatory for freedmen in the South.

In concentrating on the North as a source of illustration of this moral lag on equality, I have certainly not intended to suggest that it was peculiar to the North. I have taken agreement for granted that the lag was even greater in the South and that resistance to fulfillment of the commitment was in that area even more widespread, stubborn, and effective. It *has* been my intention, however, to suggest that the default was not peculiar to the South.

When such a lag develops between popular convictions and constitutional commitments, and when that lapse cannot be conveniently rationalized by statutory or amendatory procedures, it becomes the embarrassing task of the Supreme Court of the United States to square ideals with practice, to effect a rationalization. The justices in this instance examined the words of the Fourteenth Amendment and, by what Justice John M. Harlan in a famous dissenting opinion called "subtle and ingenious verbal criticism," discovered that they did not at all mean what they seemed to mean, nor what their authors thought they meant. By a series of opinions beginning in 1873 the court constricted the Fourteenth Amendment by a narrow interpretation which proclaimed that privileges and immunities we call civil rights were not placed under federal protection at all. In effect, they found that the commitment to equality had never really been made.

The Union fought the Civil War on borrowed moral capital. With their noble belief in their purpose and their extravagant faith in the future, the radicals ran up a staggering war debt, a moral debt that was soon found to be beyond the country's capacity to pay, given the undeveloped state of its moral resources at the time. After making a few token payments during Reconstruction, the United States defaulted on the debt and unilaterally declared a moratorium that lasted more than eight decades. The country was only nominally spared the formality of bankruptcy by the injunctions of the Supreme Court that cast doubt on the validity of the debt. In the meantime, over the years, interest on the debt accumulated. The debt was further augmented by the shabby treatment of the forgotten creditors, our own Negro citizens.

Then in the middle of the twentieth century conscience finally began to catch up with commitment. Very suddenly, relatively speaking, it became clear that the almost forgotten Civil War debt had to be paid, paid in full, and without any more stalling than was necessary. As in the case of the commitment to emancipation during the Civil War, amoral forces and pressures such as the exigencies of foreign propaganda, power politics, and military necessities exercised a powerful influence upon the recommitment to equality. But also as in the case of emancipation, the voices of conscience, of national creed, and of religious conviction played their parts. In the second instance the demands of the Negroes themselves played a more important part in the pressure than before. Equality was at last an idea whose time, long deferred, had finally come.

Once again there was a lag between popular conviction and constitutional interpretation. Only this time the trend ran the opposite way, and it was the Constitution that dawdled behind conviction. Again it proved unfeasible to close the gap by statutory or amendatory procedures, and again it became the embarrassing task of the Supreme Court to effect an accommodation, a rationalization. Once more the justices scrutinized the words of the Fourteenth Amendment, and this time they discovered that those words really meant what they said, and presumably had all along. The old debt that the court had once declared invalid they now pronounced valid.

Although this was acknowledged to be a national debt,

in the nature of things it would have to be paid by a special levy that fell with disproportionate heaviness upon one section of the country. The South had been called on before to bear the brunt of a guilty national conscience. It is now called on a second time. One could hope that the South's experience in these matters might stand it in good stead, that having learned to swallow its own words before, it might do so again with better grace, that it might perform what is required of it with forbearance and humility. I do not know. I can only admit that present indications are not very reassuring.

There is no apparent prospect of full compliance nor of an easy solution. The white South is resisting, and a reactionary part of it is defiant. The resistance is stubborn. A minority could become nasty and its defiance brutish. Already there is evidence that the patience of the rest of the country is not unlimited. There is a sense of frustration and a demand that there be no more faltering. The taunts and jeers of our foreign adversaries are a provocation, and so are the partisan rivalries of politicians. The demand for stern measures and the use of armed force is growing. An example has already been set and more could follow. But the center of resistance has scarcely been seriously challenged, and when it is, the prospect is likely to grow even darker. These are facts that no one can contemplate soberly without a sense of foreboding.

We are presently approaching the centennial anniversary of the Civil War. Simultaneously we are approaching the climax of a new sectional crisis—a crisis that divides the country along much the same old sectional lines, over many of the same old sectional issues. It would be an ironic, not to say tragic, coincidence if the celebration of the anniversary took place in the midst of a crisis reminiscent of the one celebrated.

The historian who, in these circumstances, writes the commemorative volumes for the Civil War centennial would seem to have a special obligation of sobriety and fidelity to the record. If he writes in that spirit, he will flatter the self-righteousness of neither side. He will not picture the North as burning for equality since 1863 with a hard, gem-like flame. He will not picture the South as fighting for the eternal verities. He will not paint a holy war that ennobled its participants. And he will try to keep in mind the humility that prevented the central figure in the drama from ever falling in with the notion that he was the incarnation of the Archangel Michael.

5

The Political Legacy of Reconstruction

OF ALL THE REVOLUTIONARY PROPOSALS THAT EVENTUALLY received the sanction of law in the upheaval of Reconstruction, the proposal to give the freedmen the unrestricted right to vote was one of the most difficult for contemporaries to accept, in the North as well as in the South. Emancipation itself had been repeatedly disavowed as a war aim until the war was well under way. Civil rights for freedmen was another cautiously advanced afterthought. Enfranchisement came in belatedly, surreptitiously, almost disingenuously advanced by its proponents, grudgingly accepted by a North that moved under duress and the argument of necessity and greeted with gloomy forebodings of failure, if not disaster. These attitudes were widespread, and they were not confined to copperheads, doughfaces, and mossback conservatives.

Representative of the skeptical and negative attitude of the time is the following pronouncement: "When was it ever known that liberation from bondage was accompanied by a recognition of political equality? Chattels personal may be instantly translated from the auction-block into freemen; but when were they ever taken at the same time to the ballot-box, and invested with all political rights and immunities? According to the laws of development and progress, it is not practicable. . . . Nor, if the freed blacks were admitted to the polls by Presidential fiat, do I see any permanent advantage likely to be secured by it; for, submitted to as a necessity at the outset, as soon as the state was organized and left to manage its own affairs, the white population, with their superior intelligence, wealth, and power, would unquestionably alter the franchise in accordance with their prejudices, and exclude those thus summarily brought to the polls. Coercion would gain nothing."

The author of these sentiments, written in 1864, was none other than William Lloyd Garrison of the *Liberator,* the man who swore to be "harsh as truth and uncompromising as justice." Nor was he alone among the abolitionists in these sentiments, for the radicals themselves were divided on the matter of Negro suffrage. Even Senator Charles Sumner, one of the earlier and most powerful advocates of placing the ballot in the freedman's hands, was prepared in a Senate speech on February 5, 1866, to admit that educational qualifications for the suffrage would be advisable. At that time, of course, educational restrictions, even a literacy test fairly administered, would have limited the franchise to a small minority of the freedmen. Horace Greeley of the New York *Tribune,* an old friend of the slave, would "limit the voting privilege to the competent and deserving" and suggested such qualifications as ability to read and write, payment of taxes, or establishment in a trade. General O. O. Howard, head of the Freedmen's Bureau, hoped that the franchise would be limited "at least by an educational qualification." This far, of course, President Lincoln and President Johnson were prepared to go, and both in fact did unsuccessfully recommend to Southern states such franchise laws.

To go further than that in 1866 or even later was to incur grave political risks, that even the most radical of Republicans were reluctant to assume. Only five states in the North, all with a negligible percentage of colored population, provided for Negro franchise. In 1865 Wisconsin, Minnesota, and Connecticut defeated proposals to allow the Negroes to vote, and the Nebraska constitution of 1866 confined suffrage to whites. New Jersey and Ohio in 1867 and Michigan and Pennsylvania in 1868 turned down proposals for Negro suffrage. Dr. W. E. B. Du Bois, who contends that in 1861 "probably not one white American in a hundred believed that Negroes could become an integral part of American democracy," concludes that even by 1868 "the country was not ready for Negro suffrage."

Yet Negro suffrage did come. It came very quickly. In fact, by 1868 it had already come in the South. How it came and why are important determinants in the political legacy left the South and the American Negro by Reconstruction.

Thaddeus Stevens, foremost champion of the freedmen, master of the Republican House majority, and leader of Radical Reconstruction, was advocating some extremely radical measures. He was quite ready to disfranchise Southern whites in great numbers and to confiscate great quantities of their land. "It is intended to revolutionize their feelings and principles," he declared. "This may startle feeble minds and shake weak nerves. So do all great improvements." To those who objected to humiliating the defeated foe, he replied: "Why not? Do not they deserve humiliation? If they do not, who does? What criminal, what felon deserves it more?"

But for all his radicalism, Stevens was not yet prepared to enfranchise the Negro freedmen. For one thing, of course, he knew that public opinion would not support it and that the majority of his own party was against it. But apart from political reasons he had other doubts about the wisdom of the measure, some of them similar to those expressed by Garrison, Greeley, Howard, and, for that matter, President Andrew Johnson.

On this vital matter Stevens, contrary to his reputation, can be classified as a moderate or conservative. For one thing he doubted that the freedmen were prepared for intelligent voting. The conditions and laws of slavery, he said on December 18, 1865, "have prevented them from acquiring an education, understanding the commonest laws of contract, or of managing the ordinary business of life." The following month, on January 31, 1866, while urging a constitutional amendment basing representation in the House on the number of qualified voters in a state, Stevens actually expressed hope that the Southern states would not immediately grant the freedmen suffrage and thereby increase Southern voting power in Congress. He assumed that the Negroes would fall under the political influence of their former masters. "I do not therefore want to grant them this privilege for some years . . . four or five years hence, when the freedmen shall have been made free indeed, when they shall have become intelligent enough, and there are sufficient loyal men there to control the representation from those States," Negro voting would be safe enough. In fact, at this time, Stevens adopted a states' rights position: "I hold that the States have the right, and always have had it, to fix the elective franchise within their own States."

Stevens' solution to the freedmen's suffrage problem was to force upon the Southern states the dilemma posed by the proposed Fourteenth Amendment. According to these terms the states would have to choose between excluding the freedmen from the ballot box, thus reducing their number of representatives to about forty-six, or on the other hand, enfranchising them, thereby increasing their representatives to about eighty-three but running the grave risk of losing control to the Republic party. To ensure the adoption of the amendment Stevens proposed that it be submitted only to the non-Southern states and declared adopted when approved by three-fourths of these states, exclusive of the South. This solution was rejected by his party, and the Southern states voted the amendment down when it was submitted to them along with the other states.

Still hesitant, still reluctant to accept immediate freedman's suffrage and impose it by force, Stevens temporized with still another proposal. This was contained in a bill he introduced on December 13, 1866, for the reconstruction of North Carolina. In this he proposed to restrict the ballot to those of both races who could read and write or who owned real estate assessed at a value of a hundred dollars or more. Loyal men who had voted before (whites) were not to be disfranchised, but certain classes of Confederates were. There was at times, as Ralph Korngold has suggested, something of Lincoln's hesitant approach to emancipation about Stevens' approach to enfranchisement. Hesitation ceased, however, early in 1867, almost two years after the war. He now went the whole way of military rule, disfranchisement of large numbers of Southern whites and immediate and universal Negro suffrage—full scale Radical Reconstruction.

Reasons for the conversion of Thaddeus Stevens will always be debated. A few facts stand out, however, with inescapable clarity. President Johnson's plan of reconstruction would have increased the Southern delegation in the House of Representatives by some thirteen members, since all the freedmen instead of three-fifths would have been counted in apportionment. Without Negro ballots it was probable that all the additional seats, plus all the rest of the seats of the eleven states, would be filled by Democrats and not Republicans. These same states would not only swell the opposition votes in Congress but the electoral votes in presidential contests. About thirty-seven of the Southern seats in the House would be accounted for by Negro population, who had no votes, and likely filled by sworn opponents of the party that took credit for Negro freedom. To ask an overwhelmingly Republican Congress —radical or conservative—to approve such a plan was to ask water to run uphill. Conservative Republicans were no more ready to commit political hara-kiri than Radical Republicans.

"Another good reason is," said Stevens in support of his plan, "it would insure the ascendancy of the Union [Republican] party. Do you avow the party purpose? exclaims some horror stricken demagogue. I do. For I believe, on my conscience, that on the continued ascendancy of that party depends the safety of this great nation. If impartial [Negro] suffrage is excluded in the rebel States then every one of them is sure to send a solid rebel [Democratic] representation to Congress, and cast a solid rebel electoral vote. They, with their kindred Copperheads [Democrats] of the North, would always elect the President and control Congress."

Stevens' follower, Roscoe Conkling of New York, was quite as blunt and more specific. "Shall one hundred and twenty-seven thousand white people in New York cast but one vote in this House and have but one voice here, while the same number of white people in Mississippi have three votes in three voices? Shall the death of slavery add two fifths to the entire power which slavery had when slavery was living? Shall one white man have as much share in the Government as three other white men merely because he lives where blacks out-number whites two to one? . . . No sir; not if I can help it."

In addition to "the party purpose" so frankly avowed by Stevens, there was another purpose which was not frankly declared. It was more often disavowed, concealed, deprecated. This was the purpose of the business community. Although there were significant divisions within the community, a powerful group saw in the return of a disaffected and Democratic South a menace to the economic order that had been established during the absence of the seceding states from the Union. On nearly every delicate and disturbing economic issue of the day—taxation, the National Bank, the national debt, government bonds and their funding, railroads and their financing, regulation of corporations, government grants and subsidies to business, protective tariff legislation—on one and all the business community recognized in the unreconstructed South an antagonist of long standing. In combination with traditional allies in the West and North, the South could upset the new order. Under these circumstances, the Northern business community, except for the banking and mercantile interests allied with the Democrats, put aside conservative habits and politics and threw its support to Radical Reconstruction.

Neither the party purpose, the business purpose, nor the two combined constituted a reputable justification with which to persuade the public to support a radical and unpopular program. But there was a purpose that *was* both reputable and persuasive—the philanthropic purpose, the argument that the freedmen needed the ballot to defend and protect their dearly bought freedom, their newly won civil rights, their welfare and livelihood. Of their philanthropic argument the Radicals could make a persuasive and cogent case. And it is undoubtedly true that some of the Radicals were motivated almost entirely by their idealism and their genuine concern for the rights and welfare of the freedmen. What is doubtful is that these were the effective or primary motives, or that they took priority over the pragmatic and materialistic motives of party advantage and sectional economic interests. It is clear at any rate that, until the latter were aroused and marshalled, the former made little progress. On the whole the skepticism of Secretary Gideon Welles would seem to be justified. "It is evident," he wrote in his diary, "that intense partisanship instead of philanthropy is the root of the movement."

This ulterior motivation, then, is the incubus with which the Negro was burdened before he was ever awakened into political life. The operative and effective motives of his political genesis were extraneous to his own interests and calculated to serve other ends. If there ever came a time when those ends—party advantage and sectional business interests—were better served in some other way, even in a way destructive of the basic political rights of the race, then the political prospects of the Negro would darken. Another incubus was the strongly partisan identifications of his political origins. The major national party of opposition took no part in those origins, regarded them as wholly inimical to its interests, and consequently felt no real commitment to the movement nor to the preservation of its fruits. If there came a time when that party was in the ascendancy, even locally, the political future of the Negro again would darken. To these evil portents should be added the strong resistance to Negro suffrage in the Northern states, the obvious reluctance and hesitance of radical leaders to commit the party to that course, and the grudging acquiescence of the North in the coercive use of it in the South.

After enfranchisement was in full effect in the Southern states, the Republican party felt obliged to give specific promise to the people of the North that they would be left free to keep the Negro disfranchised in their own states. In the Republican platform of 1868 appeared the following: "The guaranty by Congress of equal suffrage to all loyal men at the South was demanded by every consideration of public safety, of gratitude, and of justice, and must be maintained; while the question of suffrage in all loyal [non-Southern] States properly belongs to the people of those States." Only after the presidential election was over and General Grant had won did the party dare bring forward the Fifteenth Amendment denying the right of any state to disfranchise the Negro, and not until 1870 was its ratification completed.

In the meantime a political revolution was under way in the Southern states, a revolution that is the first chapter in the history of the Negro voter in America. The initial step under military government, after the destruction of the old civil governments, was the creation of the new electorate in 1867 and 1868. In all, more than 703,000 Negroes and some 627,000 whites were registered as qualified voters in the reconstructed states. The processes of disfranchisement and enfranchisement were going on simultaneously. The number of whites disfranchised is unknown and unknowable, but it is evident from a comparison of population and registration figures that the number was rather large in some states. While only two states had a colored majority of population, five states were given a colored majority of registered voters. The male population of voting age in Louisiana in 1860 was 94,711 whites and 92,502 Negroes, but only 45,218 whites were registered as against 84,436 Negroes. Alabama's voting age population in 1860 was 113,871 whites and 92,404 Negroes, but only 61,295 whites were registered against 104,518 Negroes. While some states with white majorities in population were given colored majorities in their electorate, others had their white majorities drastically reduced, and the two states with a preponderance of Negroes in population, South Carolina and Mississippi, had overwhelming majorities of colored voters.

This new-born electorate of freedmen was plunged immediately into action by the election of delegates to constitutional conventions. They followed by electing legislative bodies, state and local officials, and by full-scale and continuous participation in all phases and aspects of political life in a period that was abnormally active in a political way. To characterize the quality of the performance of this many people over a decade of time and in a multiplicity of activities with sweeping adjectives, "good" or "bad" or "indifferent," would be to indulge in empty generalities. That the mass of these people had less education, less experience in public affairs, and less property of all sorts than the white voters is obvious. As for the more intangible endowments of status and inner security that the psychologists stress, their relative impoverishment was appalling, unprecedented among American or any other

known electorates. Their very appearance at the polls in
mass, wearing the rags of slave days and bearing the
ancient stigmata of oppression, conjured up every gloomy
prognostication of the fate of democracies from Aristotle
to the Federalists. Not Athens, nor Rome, nor Paris at
greatest turbulence had confronted their like. Here was
the Federalist beast who would turn every garden into a
pigsty. Here was old John Adams' shiftless and improvi-
dent Demos, pawn of demagogues and plutocrats and
menace to all order. Here in the flesh was Hamilton's "tur-
bulent and changing" mass who "seldom judge or deter-
mine right" and who made it necessary to give to "the rich
and well born" that "distinct, permanent share in the
government," which alone would insure stability. Here
was the ultimate test of the democratic dogma in the most
extreme form ever attempted.

The records left by that revolutionary experiment have
been widely used to discredit both the experiment itself
and democratic faith in general. Yet those records need
not put democracy out of countenance, nor are they wholly
devoid of comfort for those of that faith. No red glow of
anarchy lit up the southern horizon as a consequence of
the revolution, and the enfranchised freedmen did not
prove the unleashed beast of Federalist imagination. Moral
pigsties undoubtedly developed, but they were oftener
than not the creation of the other race, and more of them
were to be found outside the South than within.

The new electorate of freedmen proved on the whole
remarkably modest in their demands, unaggressive in their
conduct, and deferential in their attitude. In no state did

they hold place and power in anything approaching their actual numbers and voting strength. The possible exception was South Carolina, and there they held a majority of seats only in the lower house of the legislature. In the first legislature under the new constitution of Mississippi, the other state with a large Negro majority of population, Negro representatives constituted only two-sevenths of the membership of the House and an even smaller proportion of the Senate. Freedmen of that state almost never took advantage of their numbers to seize control in local government, for a Negro majority in a municipal government seems to have been unknown. There was only one Negro mayor of a city in the state and a record of only twelve sheriffs. Only three Negroes were elected in the whole country to the Forty-first Congress, the first to which they were eligible, and there were never more than eight at one time out of a total of more than one hundred members from the Southern states. In view of the subordinate role and the few offices that the freedmen took, no state in the South could properly be said to have been under Negro rule or "domination" at any time.

Yet in varying numbers and different states Negroes occupied all the varieties of public office in existence, up to but not including the governorship. They served as policemen and supreme court justices, recorders of deeds and lieutenant-governors, sheriffs and prosecuting attorneys, justices of the peace and state superintendents of education, mayors and United States senators. Without doubt some of them made awkward efforts and a few of them cut some grotesque capers, but upon the crude stage of frontier democracy comic figures had appeared before this time, and none of them could have been taken for colored minstrels before 1868. In an age of low public morals the country over, some of the neophyte politicians were as guilty of corruption as the old hands, but the neophytes rarely seem to have received their fair share of graft.

In retrospect, one is more impressed with the success that a people of such meager resources and limited experience enjoyed in producing the number of sober, honest, and capable leaders and public servants they did. The appearance of some of this sort in every state is the main comfort the record provides to the democratic faith. They give the impression of people struggling conscientiously under desperate odds to live up to a test such as no other people had ever been subjected to in all the long testing of the democratic theory. Their success varied from state to state. With regard to Mississippi the conclusions of Vernon Wharton are that "altogether, as governments go, that supplied by the Negro and white Republicans in Mississippi between 1870 and 1876 was not a bad government. Never, in states, counties, or towns, did the Negroes hold office in proportion to their numbers. . . . The Negroes who held county offices were often ignorant, but under the control of white Democrats or Republicans they supplied a form of government which differed little from that in counties where they held no offices. The three who represented the state in Congress were above reproach. Those in the legislature sought no special advantages for their race, and in one of their very first acts they petitioned Congress to remove all political disabilities from the whites. With their white Republican colleagues, they gave to the state a government of greatly expanded functions at a cost that was low in comparison with that of almost any other state."

By the operation of a sort of historical color bar, the history of the Negro's political experience in Reconstruction has been studied too much in isolation and pictured as unique. There were unique features in that history, of course, but it does not constitute the only, nor the last, instance of the sudden enfranchisement of large numbers of politically inexperienced people. Nor does it support the stereotype of the Negro as the political tyro and neophyte of the western world, the laggard in the race for political maturity. After the Reconstruction episode was over, millions of people entered this country. Of the more than twelve million white immigrants who poured into the stream of American citizenship in the fifty years after 1880 from southern and eastern European countries, it is doubtful that more than a very small percentage had ever enjoyed any significant experience of direct political participation in the democratic sense. Their first taste of such experience came in the 1880's, the 1890's, or 1900's, or later when they took out citizenship papers. Here were the real political neophytes of the American electorate. They greatly outnumber the Negro population. They too were dominated by bosses and influenced by handouts and small favors. The record of the inexperience, naïveté, and ineptitude of these erstwhile peasants in the big city slums is written in the history of corrupt city bosses, rings, and machines, a history that can match some of the darker chapters of Reconstruction government. The Mugwump reformers turned against them, as they turned against the Radical Republicans, because of the corruption associated with their regimes. Eventually the immigrants learned the ropes, gained experience and assurance, helped clean up some of the messes their inexperience had created, and gained acceptance as respected members of the body politic.

The immigrants had their own handicaps of language and prejudice to deal with, but they never had anything approaching the handicaps against which the Negro had to struggle to gain acceptance. The prejudices that the immigrants confronted were nothing like the race prejudice with which the Negro had to cope. Nor was the white immigrant's enfranchisement accompanied by the disfranchisement of the ruling and propertied classes of the community in which he settled. Neither did the exercise of his franchise have to be protected by the bayonets of federal troops, nor did the gaining of his political rights appear to old settlers as a penalty and punishment inflicted upon them, a deliberate humiliation of them by their conquerors. Political leaders of the immigrants were not ordinarily regarded by the old settlers as "carpetbaggers," intruders, and puppets of a hostile government sent to rule over them; immigrants did not regard the old settlers as their former owners, any more than the old settlers looked upon the immigrants as their former slaves. The situation of the latest political neophytes was, after all, in many ways quite different from that of the neophytes of the seventies.

The time eventually came when the incubus of their political genesis returned to haunt the freedmen and de-

stroy their future. That was the time when the two dominant operative motives of Radical Reconstruction, party
advantage and sectional business interests, became in-
active—the time when it became apparent that those
mighty ends could better be served by abandoning the experiment and leaving the freedmen to shift for themselves.
The philanthropic motive was still a factor, and in many
minds still strong, but it was not enough without the support of the two powerful props of party advantage and
sectional interests. The moment of collapse came at different times in different states, but the climax and consolida-
tion of the decision came with the disputed presidential
election of 1876 and the settlement that resolved it in the
Compromise of 1877.

It would be neither fair nor accurate to place all the
blame upon the North and its selfish interests. There had
been plenty of willing co-operation on the part of Southern whites. They had used craft and guile, force and violence, economic pressure and physical terror, and all the
subtle psychological devices of race prejudice and propaganda at their command. But the Southern whites were
after all a minority, and not a strong minority at that. The
North had not only numbers and power on its side, but
the law and the Constitution as well. When the moment
of crisis arrived, however, the old doubts and skepticism
of the North returned, the doubts that had kept the Negro
disfranchised in the North after freedman's suffrage had
been imposed upon the South. After the Fifteenth Amendment was passed, the North rapidly lost interest in the
Negro voters. They were pushed out of the limelight by

other interests, beset by prejudices, and neglected by politicians. The Northern Negro did not enjoy a fraction of the political success the Southern Negro enjoyed, as modest as that was. Reformers and Mugwumps of the North identified corruption with the Radical wing of the Republican party, lost interest in the Negro allies of the Radicals, and looked upon them as a means of perpetuating corrupt government all over the nation as well as in the South. In this mood they came to the conclusion that the Negro voter had been given a fair chance to prove his worth as a responsible citizen and that the experiment had proved a failure. This conclusion appeared in many places, most strangely perhaps in the columns of that old champion of the race, the New York *Tribune* (April 7, 1877), which declared that the Negroes had been given "ample opportunity to develop their own latent capacities," and had only succeeded in proving that "as a race they are idle, ignorant, and vicious."

The North's loss of faith in its own cause is reflected in many surprising places. One example must suffice. It is of special interest because it comes from the supreme official charged with enforcing the Fifteenth Amendment and guaranteeing to the freedmen their political rights, the President whose administration coincided with Radical Reconstruction and the whole great experiment—General U. S. Grant. According to the diary of Secretary Hamilton Fish, entry of January 17, 1877: "He [Grant] says he opposed the Fifteenth Amendment and thinks it was a mistake, that it had done the Negro no good, and had been a hindrance to the South, and by no means a political advantage to the North."

During the present struggle for Negro rights, which might be called the Second Reconstruction—though one of quite a different sort—I have noticed among Negro intellectuals at times a tendency to look back upon the First Reconstruction as if it were in some ways a sort of Golden Age. In this nostalgic view that period takes the shape of the race's finest hour, a time of heroic leaders and deeds, of high faith and firm resolution, a time of forthright and passionate action, with no bowing to compromises of "deliberate speed." I think I understand their feeling. Reconstruction will always have a special and powerful meaning for the Negro. It is undoubtedly a period full of rich and tragic and meaningful history, a period that should be studiously searched for its meanings, a period that has many meanings yet to yield. But I seriously doubt that it will ever serve satisfactorily as a Golden Age—for anybody. There is too much irony mixed with the tragedy.

6

A Southern Critique for the Gilded Age

Melville, Adams, and James

ONE TRADITIONAL MEANS THE SOUTH EMPLOYED FOR DE-
fining its identity and keeping the image clear was the
running critique of Yankee morals it kept going over the
years. It was not invariably on the receiving end of social
criticism and moral attack. The crudities, excesses, and
shams of the Gilded Age presented Southern critics and
moralists with the broadest target they had ever had above
the Potomac. Yet this opportunity coincided ironically
with the lowest ebb of Southern influence and confidence.
A few isolated spokesmen of the old critique of Yankee
"progress" nevertheless pressed the attack with enfeebled
forces. The anonymous author of an essay entitled "The
Age of Sham" in *De Bow's Review* of 1868 typified the
scorn with which the Southern school greeted the new
industrial civilization. "Alas!" he wrote, "we have sham
idols, sham heroes, sham politicians, sham scholars, and
sham schools." The whole age was gilded with a "false

glitter, the pale mockery of the pure gold of truth, honor, and religion."

In like vein George Fitzhugh, George Frederick Holmes, Albert Taylor Bledsoe, Robert L. Dabney, and other champions of the Lost Cause continued to pronounce judgment upon the shortcomings of the new Yankee order. The combined impact of their criticism could scarcely have been more infinitesimal. Discredited from the outset, they could be readily dismissed as embittered die-hards, hopelessly outmoded, and their criticism labeled proslavery propaganda. The only Southern spokesmen who commanded national attention in that era were those of the New South school, who swelled the chorus in praise of the new order.

One of the most curious phenomena in the intellectual history of the period was that it remained for *Northern* writers, three of the most discerning critics of the age, to acknowledge the relevance of the Southern tradition and bring to bear that point of view in their critique of American society. They were Herman Melville, Henry Adams, and Henry James. Each came of an authentic Yankee heritage.

Melville employed this point of view in his long narrative and philosophical poem *Clarel* (1876), Adams in his satirical novel *Democracy* (1880), and James in his novel *The Bostonians* (1886). In each of these works a Southerner, a veteran of the Confederate Army, is introduced in a sympathetic role. His importance varies with the work concerned, but in each of the three works the Southerner serves as the mouthpiece of the severest stric-

tures upon American society or, by his actions or character, exposes the worst faults in that society. He does not
necessarily express the author's views, but the views he
does express and the tradition he represents are assured
a sympathetic reception.

I

In December, 1866, Herman Melville received an ap-
pointment as an outdoor inspector for the New York Customhouse. His office was on a North River wharf not far
from his home, and his wages were four dollars a day. He
kept the job for nineteen years. Forty-seven at the time he
accepted the customhouse place, Melville was already past
his literary prime and rapidly fading from public notice.
In a letter written in 1872 pleading that Melville's job be
spared from the spoilsmen, his brother-in-law pictured the
poet in his strange environment. "Surrounded by low
venality," he wrote, "he puts it all quietly aside,—quietly
returning money which has been thrust into his pockets
behind his back, avoiding offense alike to the corrupting
merchants and their clerks and runners, who think that
all men can be bought, and to the corrupt swarms who
shamelessly seek their price;—quietly, steadfastly doing
his duty, and happy in retaining his own self-respect." It
was from this vantage point that Melville viewed the sordid postwar scene, and it was here, between 1870 and 1876,
that he wrote his long poem *Clarel*.
Social criticism is only an incidental and belatedly in-

troduced theme of the four-thousand-line poem. The major theme is the quest of the American youth Clarel for philosophical meanings. No Faustian figure, no demon-driven Ahab, Clarel is a man plagued by doubts and yearning for a tenable faith, torn between the will to believe and the impulse of skepticism. The narrative deals with a pilgrimage in the Holy Land, where Melville had traveled in 1857, and is full of problems of faith and skepticism treated earlier by Tennyson and Arnold. The argument is developed by conversations among Clarel, three other Americans, and numerous characters from other lands representing different faiths and philosophies. One of the most attractive and persuasive characters in the entourage is Derwent, an Anglican priest, a gentleman, and a thoroughly articulate Christian. Derwent found no difficulty in countering the skepticism of the less sophisticated Clarel and hedging in his arguments with doctrines of liberalism, progress, and optimism. While Clarel could not handle the arguments of his friend, he chafed impotently against what he dimly felt to be their essential complacency, even their smugness. To counter Derwent's philosophy, and one suspects to voice his own smoldering rage as well, Melville introduces the expatriate Confederate soldier Ungar.

Ungar is pictured not only as a Southern rebel but as a Southerner with Indian blood in his veins, descendant of a union between one of Calvert's cavaliers and "a wigwam maid" of Maryland. He has "an Anglo brain, but Indian heart." He is loyal to the Lost Cause, but holds slavery "a grief" and "an iniquity." He rides apart from his countrymen, taking no part at first in their discussions, and for a

long time remaining a subject of speculation and a figure
of mystery.

> His shoulders lithe
> Were long-sloped and yet ample, too,
> In keeping with each limb and thew:
> Waist flexile as a willow withe;
> Withal, a slouched reserve of strength,
> As in the pard's luxurious length;
> The cheek, high-boned, of copperish show
> Enhanced by sun on land and seas;
> Long hair, much like a Cherokee's,
> Curving behind the ear in flow
> And veiling part a sabre-scar
> Slant on the neck, a livid bar;
> Nor might the felt hat hide from view
> One temple pitted with strange blue
> Of powder-burn. Of him you'd say—
> A veteran, no more. But nay:
> Brown eyes, what reveries they keep—
> Sad woods they be, where wild things sleep. . . .
> A native of the fair South-west—
> Their countryman, though of a zone
> Varied in nature from their own:
> A countryman—but how estranged!

As a Confederate veteran and as a Southerner of Indian
heritage, Ungar is an American who has suffered two re-
jections, two defeats, and a double estrangement from his
native land. Bearing the scars of Antietam and Gettysburg,
he has fled "the immense charred solitudes" of the war-
burnt and devastated South and voluntarily entered the

service of the Turks as a mercenary soldier. In the presence of this somber and forbidding figure, optimistic talk of progress and justice turns to cant in the mouth of the kindly priest. Whether Ungar speaks as a Southerner or as part-Indian—and he speaks sometimes as one and sometimes as the other—his heritage of multiple grievances lends both motivation and authority to his bitter pronouncements upon contemporary civilization.

Ungar's first Jeremiad is prompted by the proverb, "as cruel as a Turk." He reminds Derwent that it was originated in the time of the crusades by the Anglo-Saxons, the same race that deprived the Confederacy of medicine by blockade. He continues:

> The Anglo-Saxons—lacking grace
> To win the love of any race;
> Hated by myriads dispossessed
> Of rights—the Indians East and West.
> These pirates of the sphere! grave looters—
> Grave, canting Mammonite freebooters,
> Who in the name of Christ and Trade
> (Oh, bucklered forehead of the brass!)
> Deflowered the world's last sylvan glade!

This "wandering Ishmael from the West" continued to exasperate his companions by scoffing at the idea of progress, defending the Middle Ages, and denouncing the works of capitalism. Some of them decide he is "a man of bitter blood," perverse for the sheer sake of perversity. Ungar is as harsh and unsparing in his exposure of the hypocrisies of "equality," the cruelties of "free enterprise,"

and the evils of wage slavery as ever George Fitzhugh or
John Calhoun contrived to be. Democracy is the "Arch-
strumpet of an impious age." He will concede nothing
to the optimist who cites the advance of arts and sciences
as the hope of the future:

> Your arts advance in faith's decay:
> You are but drilling the new Hun
> Whose growl even now can some dismay;
> Vindictive in his heart of hearts,
> He schools him in your mines and marts—
> A skilled destroyer.

Rolfe, one of the Americans, protests vigorously that,
while Ungar's pessimism might find justification in the
dark future of the Old World, the hope of mankind lay
in the New World. There free land and the open frontier
provided a providential safety valve to release men from
the bitter conflicts that plague the rest of the world. In
Rolfe's words:

> The vast reserves—the untried fields;
> These long shall keep off and delay
> The class-war, rich-and-poor-man fray
> Of history. From these alone
> Can serious trouble spring. Even that
> Itself, this good result may own—
> The first firm founding of the state.

Ungar would have none of this flattering unction of
nationalism. Far from an exception, America's polyglot,
materialistic society was more susceptible to the modern
forces of disintegration and brutalization than other parts

of the world. In framing the Southerner's reply to Rolfe, Herman Melville in all probability penned the blackest commentary on the future of his country ever written by an American in the nineteenth century:

> Yours seem a reasonable tone;
> But in the New World things make haste;
> Not only men, the *state* lives fast—
> Fast breeds the pregnant eggs and shells,
> The slumberous combustibles
> Sure to explode. 'Twill come, 'twill come!
> One demagogue can trouble much:
> How of a hundred thousand such?
> And universal suffrage lent
> To back them with brute element
> Overwhelming? What shall bind these seas
> Of rival sharp communities
> Unchristianized? . . .
>   Know
> Whatever happen in the end,
> Be sure 'twill yield to one and all
> New confirmation of the fall
> Of Adam. Sequel may ensue,
> Indeed, whose germs one now may view:
> Myriads playing pygmy parts—
> Debased into equality:
> In glut of all material arts
> A civic barbarism may be:
> Man disennobled—brutalized
> By popular science—atheised
> Into a smatterer . . .
>   Yet knowing all self need to know

In self's base little fallacy;
Dead level of rank commonplace:
An Anglo-Saxon China, see,
May on your vast plains shame the race
In the Dark Ages of Democracy.

2

Late one night in July, 1868, the Cunard steamer *China* sailed into New York Harbor with Henry Adams, his father and other members of the family, returning to their native land after an absence of seven years abroad. The ship anchored, and the Adamses clambered over the side into a government tugboat, which, according to Henry's account in *The Education,* "set them ashore in black darkness at the end of some North River pier."

Adams described himself as Melville, who was nearly twenty years his senior, might with more reason have done as "a survivor from the fifties." Postwar America had moved off swiftly on a new course and left him behind, "a flotsam or jetsam of wreckage," he added with a characteristic flourish of exaggeration—"a belated reveller, or a scholar-gipsy like Matthew Arnold's. His world was dead." He deemed himself no better off "than the Indians or the buffalo who had been ejected from their heritage by his own people."

Within three months after his return Adams had moved to Washington and made a successful start in a career of journalism. His specialty was exposure, and as the Grant administration developed, the rich variety of things to be exposed multiplied too fast to permit any journalist to keep pace. The young writer moved from one scandal to the next, seeking to learn whether there were any limit to the depth of degradation into which American democracy was sinking. He was sure that "Grant's administration outraged every rule of ordinary decency," and he later concluded that "one might search the whole list of Congress, Judiciary, and Executive during the twenty-five years 1870 to 1895, and find little but damaged reputation."

Disgusted with the scene after two years, Adams withdrew to teach history at Harvard from 1870 to 1877. In the latter year, however, after marrying and resigning his position, he returned to Washington. There he established his home on Lafayette Square opposite the White House, resumed his role as spectator, and continued his ruminations about the fate of democracy. His main intellectual activity in the years that followed was devoted to writing his big history of the Jefferson and Madison administrations. Although he had given up journalism, he had never lost the journalist's absorption in the current scene and his urge to express himself on the subject. In the mature Adams this urge found expression in the novel *Democracy,* which he published anonymously in 1880.

The protagonist of the novel is Mrs. Lightfoot Lee, a wealthy and sophisticated native of Philadelphia, thirty years of age and quite attractive. She had lost her husband, a descendant of one branch of the Virginia Lees who had drifted to New York, and her only child. The

ordeal of tragedy had left her, so she thought, "pure steel."
Mrs. Lee had read "voraciously and promiscuously" but
had found solace neither in German philosophy nor in
the amusements of the international set in which she
moved. In her restlessness and discontent she decides to
move to Washington to explore the secrets of power. As
Adams describes her motives, "She wanted to see with
her own eyes the action of primary forces; to touch with
her own hand the massive machinery of society; to measure
with her own mind the capacity of the motive power. She
was bent upon getting to the heart of the great American
mystery of democracy and government." The author hints
that her curiosity was not wholly disinterested. "What she
wanted," he adds, "was Power."

Mrs. Lee moved to Washington with her sister Sybil
Ross and rented a house on Lafayette Square in what
would seem to have been December, 1876, about the time
the Henry Adamses took the same step. What follows, according to Adams' biographer Ernest Samuels, "is little
more than veiled autobiography, the life and opinions of
Henry Adams and his Washington circle in 1878–79."
Madeleine Lee, who bore some resemblance to Marian
Adams, quickly attracted an exclusive salon made up of
kindred spirits and a few specimens of a different sort
carefully selected for close study.

Among the latter type admitted to her salon is Senator
Silas P. Ratcliffe of Illinois, dictator of his party and am-
bitious to become President. He had recently missed the
nomination by three votes, and he was at the moment
engaged in bringing the President-elect completely under

his power. He combined some of the traits of Senator James G. Blaine with some of the characteristics of Senator Roscoe Conkling. The press stood in awe of "the Prairie Giant from Peonia," and so did other powerful forces of society. Senator Ratcliffe presents Madeleine Lee with an opportunity for satisfying not only her curiosity but her ambition. For the Senator not only stands very close to "the great American mystery of democracy and government" that Mrs. Lee is trying to solve, but he is also looking for a wife.

For all the mastery and power he attributes to Ratcliffe, Adams paints a highly unattractive picture of the Senator. Fifty years of age, he is at the peak of his political power and prestige. Born and educated in New England, he moved West and "fresh from that hot-bed of abolition, . . . threw himself into the anti-slavery movement in Illinois," where "after a long struggle he rose with the wave." He is "a handsome man and still in his prime," but there is "a certain coarse and animal expression about the mouth, and an indefinable coldness in the eye." * An avowed cynic about reform and morality in politics, Ratcliffe undertakes to persuade Madeleine Lee of the essential correctness and inevitability of his Machiavellian code.

---

* In his essay "The Great Secession Winter of 1860–61," written in 1861, Adams described Senator Stephen A. Douglas of Illinois as a "coarse politician" with "animal features." The extent of the historian's involvement in partisan rivalries and the effect upon his judgment are suggested by his further statement that "no man in the whole nation has done so much as he [Douglas] to degrade the standard of political morality and to further the efforts of the slave power."

All that stands in the way of Ratcliffe's conquest of the
mind and heart of Mrs. Lee as it turns out in the end is
John Carrington, Virginian. In marked contrast with the
portrait of Ratcliffe, Adams' picture of Carrington is colored with great warmth and sympathy. A distant kins-
man of her husband, Carrington was accepted as friend
and mentor by Madeleine Lee from the start, because he
was "a man whom she liked, and because he was one whom
life had treated hardly." He was "of that unfortunate
generation in the south which began existence with civil
war," and he had fought four years in the Confederate
Army. Madeleine's sister Sybil sees him as a man who "had
grown used to the shocks of fate, so as to walk with calm-
ness into the face of death, and to command or obey with
equal indifference." And Madeleine herself, who "trusted
in him by instinct," declared that "he is my idea of George
Washington at thirty." The association of Carrington with
Washington is deliberate, and to emphasize the point the
novelist has another lady refer to him later, only half in
jest, as "General Washington restored to us in his prime."

A lagging law practice leaves Carrington plenty of time
to serve Mrs. Lee, of whom he soon becomes secretly
enamored, as guide through national politics. Ratcliffe is
ready with his suggestions as well. The charming explorer
of the Washington jungle concludes that she needs all the
help she can get when she contemplates "this maze of personal intrigue, this wilderness of stunted natures where
no straight road was to be found, but only the tortuous
and aimless tracks of beasts and things that crawl." Both
the horror and the fascination of the spectacle grow upon

her as she learns more of "the illiterate swarm" of congressmen, watches "the dance of democracy round the president," tests "the quagmire of politics," and attempts to sound the depths of "this ocean of corruption."

Across the Potomac, in striking contrast to the city built in swamps and sunk in quagmires of corruption, rise the stately white Virginia mansions of Arlington and Mount Vernon. They constitute a grave and silent censure of the scene below, and it is to these vantage points on the Virginia bank of the river that the novelist has his characters repair for their deeper colloquies on the future of democracy. On a picnic at Mount Vernon, Mrs. Lee sighs over the peace and dignity of the old place and exclaims, "And yet that dreadful Capitol and its office-seekers are only ten miles off." A flippant debutante tries a bit of modern irreverence at the expense of the old hero, but Nathan Gore, the only New Englander present, breaks into an impassioned tribute. He admits that Washington cared little for New England but declares that "for all that, we idolize him. To us he is Morality, Justice, Duty, Truth; half a dozen Roman gods with capital letters. He is austere, solitary, grand; he ought to be deified." Carrington, whose family "had been deep in the confidence of Washington himself," proves reticent in his comments and prefers to draw out the opinions of Senator Ratcliffe. The Senator obliges with some reflections of which Madeleine Lee takes careful note. "If Washington were President now," he observes, "he would have to learn our ways or lose his next election. . . . If virtue won't answer our purposes, we must use vice, or our opponents will put us out of office, and this was as true in Washington's day as it is now, and always will be."

Later the scene is the portico of the home of General Robert E. Lee at Arlington, where Carrington and Madeleine's sister sit one day after a pensive ride. "From the heavy brick porch they looked across the superb river to the raw and incoherent ugliness of the city." Carrington says that he would rather not go into the house, long ago gutted by looters. He explains that the Lees were old family friends and that he has memories of many happy days as a guest in the old home. Sybil is startled by "the long white ranks of head-stones, stretching up and down the hill-sides by thousands, in order of battle," and is shocked at the thought that her handsome and silent companion had borne arms against these men who had fought for her cause. In spite of this she reflects that "he gained dignity in his rebel isolation." Once again the novelist deliberately associates valor, honor, dignity, and the heroic traditions of the past—of whichever side—with Virginia soil and name and place.

In the meantime the widow continues her pursuit of "the great American mystery" and in doing so falls deeper under the powerful influence of Ratcliffe. The Senator flatters her vanity by disclosing deep secrets of state, revealing foibles of the mighty, confronting her with the moral dilemmas of the weighty decisions he is forced to make, and insisting that she apply her fine ideals to these problems, tell him what to do, and thus share the responsibility and the guilt of such compromises as he seeks to justify in her eyes. "She reconciled herself to accepting the Ratcliffian morals," we are told, "for she could see no choice. She herself had approved every step she had seen him take. She could not deny that there must be something wrong in a double standard of morality, but where was it? Mr. Ratcliffe seemed to her to be doing good work with as pure means as he had at hand. He ought to be encouraged, not reviled. What was she that she should stand in judgment?"

Another argument is silently but eloquently pressed against the widow's defenses. If she is really serious about her desire to improve and reform American politics or, for that matter, in earnest about penetrating its mysteries, what better opportunity could she ask than that of becoming the wife of the most powerful politician in the country? She has had no lack of opportunities to witness the commanding power and crushing influence he wields. She has sat in the gallery and watched him sway the Senate with his eloquence, and she has seen a new President of the United States knuckle under to his influence. Madeleine Lee's resistance gradually crumbles under the assault of Ratcliffe's tactics and her own ambition for power.

John Carrington watches in horror but in relative helplessness. He regards Ratcliffe as the very "spirit of evil," a moral monster, and he has definite proof that the politician has recently sold his influence for a huge bribe. But he is restrained from using his knowledge against the corrupt Senator by two considerations. For one thing, professional ethics keep him from disclosing the evidence of Ratcliffe's guilt, since it came into his hands through the confidence of a client. For another, his own suit has been gently rejected by Mrs. Lee, and she has already flared up resentfully at his attempts to warn her against the danger she is in.

Ratcliffe has arranged the climax of his campaign to perfection. Carrington has been unwittingly maneuvered out of the scene by accepting a mission to Mexico, which the Senator has secretly arranged. Madeleine has been escorted to the peaks of social and political prestige at a colossal ball for European royalty, and at this advantageous moment Ratcliffe makes his proposal. He puts his case so forcefully and persuasively that Mrs. Lee is about won over. She promises him her answer the next day. Then in the nick of time sister Sybil springs the letter Carrington has prepared as a final resort, revealing the story of the Senator selling out to the notorious Ship Subsidy Lobby for $100,000.

Still undaunted when he is confronted with this letter, Ratcliffe defends his action with the familiar ethic of higher necessity he has advanced repeatedly. The money was necessary to buy an election that was "almost as important to the nation as the result of the war itself," since the purchased election kept the government from falling "into the blood-stained hands of rebels."

Mrs. Lee listens, fascinated, convinced that at last she has really "got to the heart of politics, so that she could, like a physician with his stethoscope, measure the organic disease." Then she realizes that her suitor "talked about virtue and vice as a man who is colour-blind talks about red and green." Here she is "face to face with a moral lunatic" who is proposing marriage so that "she could go out to the shore of this ocean of corruption, and repeat the ancient *rôle* of King Canute, or Dame Partington with her mop and pail. What was to be done with such an animal?" She settles the problem by sending the Senator packing in a blind, frustrated rage and by fleeing to Europe herself. The fable concludes with a romantic hint that the Virginia hero will yet be successful in his suit for the hand of the fair lady whom he has released from the spell of the wicked corruptionist.

3

A great part of the sport of publishing *Democracy* anonymously and keeping the secret so well lay in the fun that Henry and Marian Adams got out of listening to their friends innocently speculate about its authorship and pass uninhibited judgment on the novel's merits, or lack of them. The wife of the English historian John Richard Green, for example, wrote Mrs. Adams: "I hope you enjoyed *Democracy* as much as we did. Mr. [Henry] James looked very severe and grave over it, but I am not sure whether it was on patriotic or artistic grounds."

Neither James nor the Greens, though old friends of the Adamses, were in on the secret of the novel's authorship. There can be little doubt, however, that if Henry James really did pull a long face over *Democracy* it was not on "patriotic grounds." The expatriate novelist could hold his own with the Adamses in caustic criticism and patronizing comment on the shortcomings of American culture. In fact, when James and the Adamses gathered, either in London or Washington, Henry and Marian Adams found themselves invariably cast in the role of patriots defending their outraged fellow countrymen from James' attacks. During the novelist's visit with the Adamses at Washington in January, 1882, Adams remarked of James' fastidious disdain for the national capital that "poor Henry James thinks it revolting in respect to politics and the intrigues that surround it."

James himself was soon contemplating a novel of social criticism on America. He was at the first peak of his creative power in the eighties, determined, he said, to "do something great," and to "prove that I *can* write an American novel." With regard to the novel he did publish in 1886, he wrote: "I wished to write a very *American* tale, a tale very characteristic of our social conditions, and I asked myself what was the most salient and peculiar point in our social life. The answer was: the situation of women, the decline of the sentiment of sex, the agitation in their behalf." Once he got started on the novel in 1884 he wrote enthusiastically to his brother William: "It is a better subject than I have ever had before, and I think will be much the best thing I have done yet. It is called *The Bostonians*. I shall be much abused for the title, but it exactly and literally fits the story, and is much the best, simplest and most dignified I could have chosen."

Like Adams' *Democracy,* James' *Bostonians* had as a central figure a woman with a will to power, but there the resemblance between the two characters stopped. There could, in fact, scarcely be any sharper contrast in fiction than that between the vibrant, charming, outgoing personality of Madeleine Lee and the introverted, neurotic, and furtive personality of Olive Chancellor, the Boston reformer and champion of woman's rights. James' portrait of her is unrelieved in its harshness and totally unsympathetic in its severity. Her eyes were not merely described as green but recalled "the glitter of green ice." Her smile was not simply wan and cold but suggested "a thin ray of moonlight resting upon the wall of a prison." She had "pointed features and nervous manner" and "it was as plain as day that she was morbid." In fact, she "was subject to fits of tragic shyness, during which she was unable to meet even her own eyes in the mirror." Her fondest ambition was that "she might be a martyr and die for something." To complete the picture of this unfortunate young woman, "she had absolutely no figure," and "she was a woman without laughter." Her very existence was a denial of femininity and sex. To make the point explicit, James writes: "There are women who are unmarried by accident, and others who are unmarried by option; but Olive Chancellor was unmarried by every implication of her being. She was a spinster as Shelley was a lyric poet, or as the month of August is sultry." The figure amounted virtually to a caricature of the Boston bluestocking, radical, and reformer.

More important is Basil Ransom, Southerner, protagonist of the novel and the very antithesis of everything Olive Chancellor represents. He is described in heroic terms as "tall and lean, dressed throughout in black," a sort of Confederate Hamlet with a "superior head" fit for "a bronze

medal," a forehead that is "high and broad, and his thick
black hair, perfectly straight and glossy," is worn in "a
leonine manner." He has "magnificent eyes" that are
"dark, deep, and glowing," full of "smouldering fire."
These characteristics, says James, "might have indicated
that he was to be a great American statesman; or, on the
other hand, they might simply have proved that he came
from Carolina or Alabama." He came in fact from Mississippi, the cultural antipodes of Massachusetts, and spoke
in an accent "pervaded by something sultry and vast, something almost African in its rich basking tone, something
that suggested the teeming expanse of the cotton field,"
but in which there was "nothing vulgar or vain." Not one
to take pleasantries about his provincial origins lightly, he
replied to the chafing of a flirtatious widow, "When I dine
out I usually carry a six-shooter and a bowie knife."

The son of a wealthy planter, Ransom had "tasted all
the cruelty of defeat." He returned from the war to find
family, property, and home ruined. After a futile attempt
to make a go of the plantation, he gave up his patrimony
to mother and sisters and headed for New York to practice law, "with fifty dollars in his pocket and a gnawing
hunger in his heart." This was in the seventies, and he was
not quite thirty years old.

In what appears to have been an uncharacteristic impulse, Olive Chancellor, who was a remote cousin and a
bit younger than Ransom, invited him to visit her in Boston. Antipathy pops and crackles the length of her Back
Bay drawing room at the first contact between Bluestocking and Mississippian. "Don't you care for human

progress?" asks Miss Chancellor. The answer comes in a carefully courteous drawl: "I don't know—I never saw any." These are the opening guns of a duel that continues intermittently throughout the book. Ransom is well armed for the encounter. He is described as "a young man of first-rate intelligence" who "had read everything." His favorite moderns were de Tocqueville and Carlyle, but he had read his Comte as well and had no difficulty holding up his end of the argument.

Cultural contrasts are multiplied and cousinly amity further deteriorates at a meeting of Boston reformers consisting of woman's-rights people, mesmerists, spiritualists, utopians, and faded abolitionists. Ransom is all ears and repressed hilarity at his opportunity to observe these specimens in their native habitat. The gaunt hall designed for plain living and high thinking is presided over by Miss Birdseye, whom Miss Chancellor admires as "one of the earliest, one of the most passionate, of the old Abolitionists," and whom James describes as "a confused, entangled, inconsequent, discursive old woman, whose charity began at home and ended nowhere, whose credulity kept pace with it, and who knew less about her fellow-creatures, if possible, after fifty years of humanitary zeal, than on the day she had gone into the field to testify against the iniquity of most arrangements." *

The outstanding feature of the evening was an unrehearsed performance by a very pretty young woman named

* The author was intensely embarrassed when Elizabeth Peabody, Hawthorne's sister-in-law, was taken to be the original of Miss Birdseye.

Verena Tarrant, who had a strange gift for "inspirational" speaking. Her father, a mesmeric healer, was the prototype of "the detested carpetbagger . . . false, cunning, vulgar, ignoble; the cheapest kind of human product," and her mother, the daughter of the most famous of the Boston abolitionists. "Want to try a little inspiration?" her father would ask and, by laying on of pallid hands, would induce one of Verena's trances. Fascinated by the girl and captivated by her performance, Olive Chancellor determines immediately to rescue Verena from her impossible parents, take the girl into her own home, and see that her queer talent and her whole life are dedicated to promoting a strange brand of feminism. Verena moves in with Olive, and there begins what James calls "one of those friendships between women which are so common in New England." Olive's proposal was: "Will you be my friend, my friend of friends, beyond every one, everything, forever and forever?" One of their embraces is interrupted by an intruder who remarks, "You ladies better look out, or you'll freeze together."

Basil Ransom is equally captivated by Verena but plans a very different future for her. He is convinced that she is "made for love," his own kind of traditional, domestic, male-dominated, familial love, and that he must rescue her from the perverse sexuality of his cousin and from the quackery of the woman's-rights lecture platform. There ensues a struggle between the Mississippian and the Bostonian for the future of Verena which is comparable to the struggle between the Virginian and the Midwesterner over Madeleine Lee, except that Verena is a more passive participant and the strange courtship is carried on in sociological rather than in political terms.

Ransom's defense of marriage, family, tradition, and chivalry is a merciless onslaught upon the cant of the age, the cant about progress, equality, universal education, and the emancipation of women. Verena has never in her life heard such irreverence about the values she has been taught to cherish, such shocking cynicism from a professed conservative. She has "never encountered such a power of disparagement or heard so much sarcasm leveled at the institutions of her country and the tendencies of the age." And all this in such mellow, exotic, and seductive cadences, that it was all the harder to resist. "She thought conservatives were only smug and stubborn and self-complacent, satisfied with what actually existed; but Mr. Ransom didn't seem any more satisfied with what existed than with what she wanted to exist, and he was ready to say worse things about some of those whom she would have supposed to be on his own side than she thought it right to say about almost anyone."

It was little wonder that in her effort to keep her influence over Verena, not to mention her self-respect, Olive Chancellor "made up her mind that there was no menace so great as the menace of Basil Ransom." She lectured the wavering Verena upon "male grossness" and reminded her of the pathos of "the bullied wives, the stricken mothers, the dishonored, deserted maidens," all the woes of womanhood at male hands. "I'll tell you what is the matter with you," she says to Verena, "—you don't dislike men as a class." Verena admitted as much and finally agreed to be spirited away beyond the reach of Ransom while she rehearses for the great event Olive had prepared, her debut as a woman's-rights wonder-worker before a vast audience of Bostonians.

In the final scene, all Boston waits for Verena in the Music Hall with growing impatience. When she does not appear, the audience bursts out in hisses and catcalls for Olive Chancellor. Backstage, in the meantime, the ardent Mississippian finally persuades Verena to throw over Olive, woman's rights, mesmerism, Boston, and the impatient Music Hall audience and flee it all with him. He whisks her away from the mob somewhat unromantically in a horse car.

The last touch of irony is not the only one by which James acknowledges that his young hero does not always stay safely this side of the preposterous. But before concluding, the novelist puts one speech in the mouth of Ransom that, for rhetorical savagery, rivals Clarel's lines on the Dark Ages of Democracy. "Mr. Ransom," declares Verena angrily, "I assure you this is an age of conscience." And he replies, "That's a part of your cant. It's an age of unspeakable shams." The trouble lies in "feminization" or in the decline of sexuality:

"The whole generation is womanized; the masculine tone is passing out of the world; it's a feminine, a nervous, hysterical, chattering, canting age, an age of hollow phrases and false delicacy and exaggerated solicitudes and coddled sensibilities, which, if we don't soon look out, will

usher in the reign of mediocrity, of the feeblest and flattest
and the most pretentious that has ever been."

4

How is one to account for the selection of a Confederate
censor for Yankee morals by three of the North's most
gifted literary figures and perceptive critics? Certainly the
answer is not to be found in any discoverable Southern
leanings or connections among them during or before
the Civil War. So far as the records reveal, all came of
Yankee forebears and, in the cases of Adams and Melville, a long line of them. Although none of the three
writers served the Union cause in a military way, all were
thoroughly loyal to that cause. Adams served it ably on
the diplomatic front and Melville in his war poems. James'
writing career did not start until after the war, but he was
a loyal patriot. None of them could claim any personal
familiarity with the South or a circle of Southern acquaintances that amounted to anything. With the exception of
Melville, who lectured as far south as Tennessee in the
mid-fifties, visited the Wilderness battle line, and paid his
respects to Grant at Culpeper, Virginia, in 1864, none of
the three had done more than set foot on Southern soil.

Yet from very early in his life the South evoked ambiva-
lent attitudes in Henry Adams. On his first contact with
a slave society at the age of twelve, when his father took
him to visit Washington in 1850, he felt both repulsion
and attraction. His first response was that of a true grand-

son of John Quincy Adams. "Slave States were dirty, un-
kempt, poverty-stricken, ignorant, vicious! He had not a
thought but repulsion for it [slavery]; and yet the picture
had another side." The other side, he speculated, might
have been "his Johnson blood," that of his grandmother,
who though born in England came of Maryland stock.
"The May sunshine and shadow had something to do
with it; the thickness of foliage and the heavy smells had
more; the sense of atmosphere, almost new, had perhaps
as much again; and the brooding indolence of a warm
climate and a negro population hung in the atmosphere
heavier than the catalpas. The impression was not simple, but the boy liked it: distinctly it remained on his
mind as an attraction, almost obscuring Quincy itself."
Memory of the trip left another long-lasting impression,
that of a carriage trip with his father over a very bad
road to visit Mount Vernon. "Bad roads meant bad morals"
to the New England mind. "The moral of this Virginia
road was clear, and the boy fully learned it. Slavery was
wicked, and slavery was the cause of this road's badness
which amounted to a social crime—and yet, at the end
of the road and product of the crime stood Mount Vernon
and George Washington."

Henry Adams had not ceased pondering the apparent
paradox of Southern wickedness producing George Washington when, more than a half century later, he was writing his *Education*. "George Washington could not be
reached on Boston lines," he reflected. "George Washington was a primary, or, if Virginians liked it better, an
ultimate relation, like the Pole Star, and amid the endless

restless motion of every other visible point in space, he alone remained steady, in the mind of Henry Adams, to the end." It was a pity, he reflected, that he had never thought to ask his father "how to deal with the moral problem that deduced George Washington from the sum of all wickedness." Clearly the problem was still on his mind while he was writing *Democracy,* but he was under no illusion that the novel had solved it.

The ambivalence of Henry Adams' attitude toward the South was matched by a similar complexity in the approach of Henry James toward Southerners and their section. James knew even fewer Southerners and less about the South than Adams or Melville. In fact he never crossed the Potomac until after his career as a novelist was finished, and his acquaintances among people of the region were casual and few in number. In a letter to William James about the weaknesses of *The Bostonians,* he complains of "the sense of knowing terribly little about the kind of life I had attempted to describe." He may have been referring in part to Boston, but after all he had lived in that city, and he had not so much as visited the South.

In his autobiographical work, *A Small Boy and Others,* James tells of the deep impression left on him as a child of ten by a family of Kentuckians named Norcom, who moved into the James' block on Washington Square in 1853. The child's imagination was stirred by "the southern glow of the Norcoms" which seemed to light up the whole community. In particular he was impressed by "the large, the lavish, ease of their hospitality," which took (for a ten-year-old) the gratifying form of free-handed dispens-

ing of sausages, johnny-cakes, and molasses. "They didn't
count and didn't grudge—the sausage-mill kept turning
and the molasses flowing for all who came." From the
safely neutral ground of New York he was already contrasting the Southern temperament with the New England character. "We were provided by their [Norcoms']
presence," he recalled, "with as happy a foil as we could
have wished to the plainness and dryness of the Wards,"
another family of friends whom he described as "all New
England." Professor Charles R. Anderson has pointed out
a marked similarity between James' description of young
Eugene Norcom who, he said, "haunted my imagination,"
and his description of Basil Ransom. As a matter of fact,
James confesses naïvely how "absurdly and disproportion-
ately" the childhood acquaintance with the Norcoms "had
helped one to 'know Southerners.'"

It is doubtful that any one of the three writers, Melville
least of all, was very seriously concerned to "know Southerners" or to bother themselves very deeply about the problem of Southern identity and heritage. What they *were*
all deeply concerned about was what had overtaken their
own society since the Civil War, the mediocrity, the crass-
ness, and the venality they saw around them. The South or
the Southern hero, past or present, was a useful foil for
the unlovely present or the symbol of some irreparable
loss. "Why do I feel unclean when I look at Mount Vernon?" asks Madeleine Lee.

Loyal Northerners all, Melville, Adams, and James are
not always able to use their Southern viewpoint with entire confidence or without some manifestations of em-

barrassment and guilt. Each takes pains to have his hero
disavow slavery, and Ransom and Carrington are made to
abandon the principle of secession as well. Thus purged
of the more troublesome doctrinal heresies, the ex-rebels
prove less of an embarrassment in polite Northern company. Adams makes Carrington a unionist who fought un-
enthusiastically for the Confederacy; James carries the
device of dissociation to the point of equivocation by referring in his own voice to the "false pride" and "moral
tinsel" of the very tradition he presents to his reader as the
standpoint from which to judge the Bostonians.

Common to the three writers was a tacit assumption
that the war really was a civil war. Its significance was
not confined to the abolition of slavery as an afterthought.
America's triumph over the South did not mean simply
the defeat of an external foe that left the victorious power
unchanged and inflicted change and revolution upon the
vanquished alone. It also meant the defeat or denial of
something within, a tradition perhaps once shared with the
fallen rebels, something that shared the downfall of the
South. In their search for what was missing in postwar
America, these Northern writers turned southward and
invoked a tradition only lately renounced.

Each of them was in some degree estranged from the
new America and rejected its dominant values. Each in
some fashion withdrew, Melville to the obscurity of the
customhouse, James to Europe as an expatriate, and
Adams to the retreat of a cynical spectator. In spite of the
disparity in their ages, each tended to identify himself
with the past, with some older period or tradition. Adams

called himself "a survivor from the fifties" whose "world was dead." James preferred the Old World and could stand the new America only in small doses. Melville could not stand much of it at any time, and it could not have cared less for him or his art.

When they came to frame their critique of the new order, they turned to the South in search of the values and traditions they had lost. Something of what they sought was really there or had been, and some of it they merely imagined. As Professor Anderson has observed, Henry James constructed a fable of Carolina as an Old World survival to which he clung to the end, and at an advanced age he sought corroboration of his fable in a tour. In the quiet old mansions of Charleston he discovered "the fallen pride of provincial palazzini," in the walled gardens he was reminded of a "little old-world quarter of quiet convents" and of the fine sense of privacy they symbolized, "One sacrificed the North on the spot." In the sea islands he imagined the "possible site of some Venice that had never mustered." He admitted the absurdity of expecting "Charleston and Savannah to betray the moral accent of Naples or Seville," but he continued his quest nevertheless.

Henry Adams was in quest of no European antiquities when he turned South, but he definitely was in search of American antiquities, the antique valor and probity of the early Republic. As a child of twelve he had decided that "Mount Vernon was only Quincy in a Southern setting. No doubt it was much more charming, but it was the same eighteenth century, the same old furniture, the same

old patriot, and the same old President." Later on he was
not so certain of the identity of Mount Vernon and Quincy.
When Madeleine Lee asks John Carrington if he regrets
the passing of the old order for which he fought, he replies: "One can't help regretting whatever it was that
produced George Washington, and a crowd of other men
like him." The problem of Mount Vernon and "the sum
of all wickedness" was still gnawing at the mind of Henry
Adams.

Among the ghosts of the Old Regime that haunted the
deep woods across the Potomac there must have been a
good deal of wry merriment from time to time over the
modern turn of events. The taste for irony could hardly
have been better served, in fact, than by the belated Yankee
deference implicit in the selection of Confederate censors
for Yankee morals.

7

The Populist Heritage and the Intellectual

THIRTY YEARS AFTER SECESSION AND CIVIL WAR, THE
South suffered a second alienation from the dominant national spirit. This received expression in the Populist upheaval of the nineties. The Populist movement won more
sympathy in the West than had the Secessionist movement.
It did not win the allegiance of as large a proportion of
Southerners as had the Lost Cause, nor did it involve those
it did win quite so deeply. But the alienation was real
enough, and the heritage it left was a lasting one.

During the long era of the New Deal, one had little
difficulty living in comparative congeniality with the Populist heritage. The two periods had much in common, and
it was easy to exaggerate the similarities and natural to seek
antecedents and analogies in the earlier era. Because of the
common setting of severe depression and economic dislo-
cation, Populism seemed even closer to the New Deal than
did Progressivism, which had a setting of prosperity. Common to both Populists and New Dealers was an antag-
onism to the values and dominant leaders of the business

community. Among both was a sense of urgency and an edge of desperation about the demand for reform. And in both, so far as the South and West were concerned, agricultural problems were the most desperate, and agrarian reforms occupied the center of attention. It seemed entirely fitting that Hugo Black of Alabama and Harry Truman of Missouri—politicians whose political style and heritage were strongly Populistic—should lead New Deal reform battles. From many points of view the New Deal was neo-Populism.

The neo-Populism of the present bred a Populistic view of the past. American historiography of the 1930's and 1940's reflects a strong persuasion of this sort. The most popular college textbook in American history was written by a Midwesterner, John D. Hicks, who was friendly to Populism and the foremost historian of the movement. The leading competitor of this book was one that shared many of the Populist leanings, even though one of its authors was a Harvard patrician and the other a Columbia urbanite. A remarkably heterogeneous assortment of men and ideas struck up congenial ties in the neo-Populist coalition. Small-town Southerners and big-city Northerners, Texas mavericks and Hudson River aristocrats, Chapel Hill liberals and Nashville agrarians were all able to discover some sort of identity in the heritage. The South rediscovered ties with the West, the farmer with labor. The New York-Virginia axis was revived. Jacksonians were found to have urban affiliations and origins. Not to be outdone, the Communists staked out claim to selected Populist heroes.

Many intellectuals made themselves at home in the neo-Populist coalition and embraced the Populist heritage. They had prepared the way for the affiliation in the twenties when they broke with the genteel tradition, adopted the mucker pose, and decided that conventional politics and the two major parties were the province of the booboc-racy and professional politicians were clowns or hypo-crites. In the thirties intellectuals made naïve identification with farmers and workers and supported their spokesmen with enthusiasm. The Populist affinity outlasted the New Deal, survived the war, and perhaps found its fullest ex-pression in the spirit of indulgent affection with which intellectuals often supported Harry Truman and his ad-ministration.

Even before Truman left the White House, however, the Populist identification fell into disgrace, and intellectuals began to repudiate the heritage. "Populist" suddenly be-came a term of opprobrium, in some circles a pejorative epithet. This resulted from no transfer of affection to Tru-man's successor, for there was very little of that among intellectuals. The origins of the altered temper came earlier.

Disenchantment of the intellectual with the masses was well under way in the forties. Mass support for evil causes in Germany and elsewhere helped to undermine the faith. The liberal's feelings of guilt and impotence were re-flected in the interest that the writings of Sören Kierke-gaard and Reinhold Niebuhr aroused, and the mood of self-flagellation was expressed in the vogue of the novels of Franz Kafka and George Orwell. The shock of the en-counter with McCarthyism sustained and intensified the mood. Liberals and intellectuals bore the brunt of the Mc-Carthyite assault on standards of decency. They were rightly alarmed and felt themselves betrayed. They were the victims of a perversion of the democracy they cherished, a seamy and sinister side of democracy to which they now guiltily realized they had too often turned a blind or indulgent eye. Stung by consciousness of their own naïveté, they responded with a healthy impulse to make up for lost time and confront their problem with all the critical resources at their command. The consequence has been a formidable and often valuable corpus of social criticism.

Not one of the critics, not even the most conservative, is prepared to repudiate democracy. There is general agreement that the fault lay in some abuse or perversion of democracy and was not inherent in democracy itself. All the critics are aware that these abuses and perversions had historic antecedents and had appeared in various guises and with disturbing frequency in national history. These unhappy tendencies are variously described as "mobism," "direct democracy," or "plebecitarianism," but there is a surprising and apparently spontaneous consensus of preference for "Populism." Although the word is usually capitalized, the critics do not as a rule limit its reference to the political party that gave currency to the term. While there is general agreement that the essential characteristics designated by the term are best illustrated by an agrarian movement in the last decade of the nineteenth century, some of the critics take the liberty of applying it to movements as early as the Jacksonians, or earlier, and to twentieth-century phenomena as well.

Reasons for this convergence from several angles upon "Populism" as the appropriate designation for an abhorred abuse are not all clear. A few, however, suggest themselves. Populism is popularly thought of as an entirely Western affair, Wisconsin as a seedbed of the movement, and Old Bob La Follette as a foremost exponent. None of these assumptions is historically warranted, but it is true that Senator McCarthy came from Wisconsin, that much of his support came from the Middle West, and that there are some similarities between the two movements. The impression of similarity has been enhanced by the historical echo of their own alarm that modern intellectuals have caught in the rather hysterical fright with which Eastern conservatives reacted to Populism in the nineties.

This essay is not concerned with the validity of recent analysis of the "radical right" and its fascistic manifestations in America. It is concerned only with the tendency to identify Populism with these movements and with the implied rejection of the Populist tradition. It is admittedly very difficult, without risk of misrepresentation and injustice, to generalize about the way in which numerous critics have employed the Populist identification. They differ widely in the meaning they attribute to the term and the importance they attach to the identification. Among the critics are sociologists, political scientists, poets, and journalists, as well as historians, and there is naturally a diversity in the degree of historical awareness and competence they command. Among points of view represented are the New Conservative, the New Liberal, the liberal-progressive, the Jewish, the Anglophile, and the urban, with some overlapping. There is no conscious spokesmen of the West or the South, but some are more or less unconscious representatives of the urban East. Every effort will be made not to attribute to one the views of another.*

Certain concessions are due on the outset. Any fairminded historian will acknowledge the validity of some of the points scored by the new critics against the Populist tradition and its defenses. It is undoubtedly true that liberal intellectuals have in the past constructed a flattering image of Populism. They have permitted their sympathy with oppressed groups to blind them to the delusions, myths, and foibles of the people with whom they sympathized. Sharing certain political and economic doctrines and certain indignations with the Populists, they have attributed to them other values, tastes, principles, and morals which the Populists did not actually share. It was understandably distasteful to dwell upon the irrational or retrograde traits of people who deserved one's sympathy and

* Daniel Bell (ed.), *The New American Right* (New York, 1955), especially essays by Richard Hofstadter, Peter Viereck, Talcott Parsons, and Seymour Martin Lipset; Edward A. Shils, *The Torment of Secrecy* (Glencoe, Ill., 1956) and "The Intellectuals and the Powers: Some Perspectives for Comparative Analysis" in *Comparative Studies in Society and History,* I (October, 1958), 5–22; Peter Viereck, *The Unadjusted Man* (Boston, 1956); Oscar Handlin, *Race and Nationality in American Life* (Boston, 1957), and "American Views of the Jews at the Opening of the Twentieth Century," *Publication of the American Jewish Historical Society,* No. 40 (June, 1951), 323–44; Richard Hofstadter, *The Age of Reform* (New York, 1955); Victor C. Ferkiss, "Ezra Pound and American Fascism," *Journal of Politics,* XVII (1955), 174–96; Max Lerner, *America as a Civilization* (New York, 1958).

shared some of one's views. For undertaking this neglected and distasteful task in the spirit of civility and forbearance which, for example, Richard Hofstadter has shown, some of the new critics deserve much credit. All of them concede some measure of value in the Populist heritage, though none so handsomely as Hofstadter, who assumes that Populism and Progressivism are strongly enough established in our tradition to withstand criticism. Others are prone to make their concessions more perfunctory and to hasten on with the job of heaping upon Populism, as upon an historical scapegoat, all the ills to which democracy is heir.

The danger is that under the concentrated impact of the new criticism the risk is incurred, not only of blurring a historical image, but of swapping an old stereotype for a new one. The old one sometimes approached the formulation that Populism is the root of all good in democracy, while the new one sometimes suggests that Populism is the root of all evil. Uncritical repetition and occasional exaggeration of the strictures of some of the critics threaten to result in establishing a new maxim in American political thought: *Radix malorum est Populismus.*

Few of the critics engaged in the reassessment of Populism and the analysis of the New American Right would perhaps go quite so far as Peter Viereck, when he writes that "beneath the sane economic demands of the Populists of 1880–1900 seethed a mania of xenophobia, Jew-baiting, intellectual-baiting, and thought-controlling lynch-spirit." Yet this far from exhausts the list of unhappy or repulsive aberrations of the American spirit that have been attributed to Populism. Other aberrations are not pictured as a "seething mania" by any one critic, but by one or another the Populists are charged with some degree of responsibility for Anglophobia, Negrophobia, isolationism, imperialism, jingoism, paranoidal conspiracy-hunting, anti-Constitutionalism, anti-intellectualism, and the assault upon the right of privacy—these among others. The Populist virus is seen as no respecter of the barriers of time or nationality. According to Edward A. Shils, "populism has many faces. Nazi dictatorship had markedly populistic features. . . . Bolshevism has a strand of populism in it too." And there was among fellow travelers a "populistic predisposition to Stalinism." On the domestic scene the strand of Populistic tradition "is so powerful that it influences reactionaries like McCarthy and left-wing radicals and great upperclass personalities like Franklin Roosevelt." And according to Viereck, Populistic attitudes once "underlay Robespierre's Committee of Public Safety" and later "our neo-Populist Committee on un-American Activities."

Among certain of the critics there is no hesitancy in finding a direct continuity between the nineteenth-century Populists and twentieth-century American fascism and Mc-Carthyism. Victor C. Ferkiss states flatly that "American fascism has its roots in American populism. It pursued the same ends and even used many of the same slogans. Both despaired of achieving a just society under the joined banners of liberalism and capitalism." His assertion supports Viereck's suggestion that "since the same impulses and resentments inspire the old Populism and the new nationalist right, let us adopt 'neo-Populism' as the proper term for the latter group." Talcott Parsons believes that "the elements of continuity between Western agrarian populism and McCarthyism are not by any means purely fortuitous," and Shils thinks the two are connected by "a straight line." It remains for Viereck to fill in the gap: "The missing link between the Populism of 1880–1900 and the neo-Populism of today—the missing link between Ignatius Donnelly and the McCarthy movement—was Father Charles Coughlin."

There is a strong tendency among the critics not only to identify Populism and the New Radical Right but to identify both with certain regions, the West and South, and particularly the Middle West. "The areas which produced the populism of the end of the nineteenth century and the early twentieth century have continued to produce them," writes Shils. Viereck puts it somewhat more colorfully: "The Bible-belt of Fundamentalism in religion mostly overlapped with the farm-belt of the Populist, Greenback, and other free-silver parties in politics. Both belts were anti-intellectual, anti-aristocratic, anti-capitalist." Parsons and Ferkiss likewise stress the regional identity of Populist-Radical Right ideology, and Viereck supplies an interesting illustration: "Out of the western Populist movement came such apostles of thought-control and racist bigotry as Tom Watson."

If so many undesirable traits are conveniently concentrated along geographical lines, it might serve a useful purpose to straighten out the political geography of Populism a bit. In the first place, as Hofstadter and other historians of the movement have noted, Populism had negligible appeal in the Middle Western states, and so did the quasi-

Populism of William Jennings Bryan. Wisconsin, Minnesota, Iowa, Illinois, and states east of them went down the line for William McKinley, Mark Hanna, gold, and the Old Conservatism (and so did Old Bob La Follette). Only in the plains states of North and South Dakota, Nebraska, and Kansas were there strong Populist leanings, and only they and the mountain states went for Bryan in 1896. At the crest of the Populist wave in 1894 only Nebraska polled a Populist vote comparable in strength to that run up in Alabama, Georgia, and North Carolina.

For the dubious distinction of being the leading Populist section, the South is in fact a strong contender; if the test used be merely quasi-Populism the pre-eminence of the former Confederacy is unchallengeable. It was easily the most solidly Bryan section of the country, and its dogged loyalty long outlasted that of the Nebraskan's native state. However, a more important test was third-party Populism, the genuine article. The remarkable strength the Populists manifested in the Lower South was gained against far more formidable obstacles than any ever encountered in the West. For there they daily faced the implacable dogmas of racism, white solidarity, white supremacy, and the bloody shirt. There was indeed plenty of "thought control and racist bigotry and lynch-spirit," but the Populists were far more often the victims than the perpetrators. They had to contend regularly with foreclosure of mortgages, discharge from jobs, eviction as tenants, exclusion from church, withholding of credit, boycott, social ostracism, and the endlessly reiterated charge of racial disloyalty and sectional disloyalty. Suspicion of loyalty was in fact *the* major psychological problem of the Southern Populists, as much so perhaps as the problem of loyalty faced by radicals of today. They contended also against cynical use of fraud comparable with any used against Reconstruction, methods that included stuffed ballot boxes, packed courts, stacked registration and election boards, and open bribery. They saw election after election stolen from them and heard their opponents boast of the theft. They were victims of mobs and lynchers. Some fifteen Negroes and several white men were killed in the Georgia Populist campaign of 1892, and it was rare that a major election in the Lower South came off without casualties.

Having waged their revolt at such great cost, the Southern Populists were far less willing to compromise their principles than were their Western brethren. It was the Western Populists who planned and led the movement to sell out the party to the Silverites, and the Southern Populists who fought and resisted the drift to quasi-Populism. The Southerners were consistently more radical, more insistent upon their economic reforms, and more stubbornly unwilling to lose their party identity in the watered-down quasi-Populism of Bryan than were the Westerners.

There is some lack of understanding about *who* the Southern Populists were for and against, as well as *what* they were for and against. Edward Shils writes that the "economic and political feebleness and pretensions to breeding and culture" of the "older aristocratic ruling class" in the South provided "a fertile ground for populistic denunciation of the upper classes." Actually the Southern Populists directed their rebellion against the newer ruling class, the industrialists and businessmen of the New South, instead of the old planters. A few of the quasi-Populists like Ben Tillman did divert resentment to aristocrats like Wade Hampton. But the South was still a more deferential society than the rest of the country, and the Populists were as ready as the railroads and insurance companies to borrow the prestige and name of a great family. The names of the Populist officials in Virginia sounded like a roll call of colonial assemblies or Revolutionary founding fathers: Page, Cocke, Harrison, Beverley, Ruffin. There were none more aristocratic in the Old Dominion. General Robert E. Lee, after the surrender at Appomattox, retired to the ancestral home of Edmund Randolph Cocke after his labors. His host was later Populist candidate for governor of the state. As the editor of their leading paper, the allegedly anglophobic Populists of Virginia chose Charles H. Pierson, an ordained Anglican priest, English by birth, Cambridge graduate, and theological student of Oxford. To be sure, the Populist leaders of Virginia were not typical of the movement in the South. But neither were Jefferson, Madison, Monroe, and John Taylor typical of *their* movement in the South: there were simply never enough aristocrats to go around. Some states had to make do with cruder customers as leaders in both Jeffersonian and Populist movements, and in the states to the west there was doubtless less habitual dependence on aristocrats, even if they had been more readily available.

In their analysis of the radical right of modern America, the new critics have made use of the concept of "status resentment" as the political motivation of their subjects.

They distinguish between "class politics," which has to do with the correction of economic deprivations, and "status politics," which has no definite solutions and no clear-cut legislative program but responds to irrational appeals and vents aggression and resentment for status insecurity upon scapegoats—usually ethnic minorities. Seymour Martin Lipset, who appears at times to include Populism in the category, has outlined the conditions typical of periods when status politics become ascendant. These are, he writes, "periods of prosperity, especially when full employment is accompanied by inflation, and when many individuals are able to improve their economic position." But the conditions under which Populism rose were exactly the opposite: severe depression, critical unemployment, and crippling currency contraction, when few were able to improve their economic position—and certainly not farmers in a cash-crop staple agriculture.

The Populist may have been bitten by status anxieties, but if so, they were certainly not bred of upward social mobility, and probably few by downward mobility either—for the simple reason that there was not much further downward for most Populists to go, and had not been for some time. Populism was hardly "status politics," and I should hesitate to call it "class politics." It was more nearly "interest politics," and more specifically "agricultural interest politics." Whatever concern the farmers might have had for their status was overwhelmed by desperate and immediate economic anxieties. Not only their anxieties but their proposed solutions and remedies were economic. While their legislative program may have often been naïve and inadequate, it was almost obsessively economic and, as political platforms go, little more irrational than the run-of-the-mill.

Yet one of the most serious charges leveled against the Populists in the reassessment of the new critics is an addiction to just the sort of irrational obsession that is typical of status politics. This is the charge of anti-Semitism. It has been documented most fully by Richard Hofstadter and Oscar Handlin and advanced less critically by others. The prejudice is attributed to characteristic Populist traits—rural provinciality, an ominous credulity, and an obsessive fascination with conspiracy. Baffled by the complexities of monetary and banking problems, Populist ideologues simplified them into a rural melodrama with Jewish international bankers as the principal villains. Numerous writings of Western Populists are cited that illustrate the tendency to use Jewish financiers and their race as scapegoats for agrarian resentment. Hofstadter points out that Populist anti-Semitism was entirely verbal and rhetorical and cautions that it can easily be misconstrued and exaggerated. He is nevertheless of the opinion "that the Greenback-Populist tradition activated most of what we have of modern popular anti-Semitism in the United States."

In the voluminous literature of the nineties on currency and monetary problems—problems that were much more stressed by silverites and quasi-Populists than by radical Populists—three symbols were repetitively used for the plutocratic adversary. One was institutional, "Wall Street," and two were ethnic, the British and Jewish bankers. Wall Street was by far the most popular and has remained so ever since among politicians of agrarian and Populistic tradition. Populist agitators used the ethnic symbols more or less indiscriminately, British along with Jewish, though some of them bore down with peculiar viciousness on the Semitic symbol. As the new critics have pointed out, certain Eastern intellectuals of the patrician sort, such as Henry and Brooks Adams and Henry Cabot Lodge, shared the Populist suspicion and disdain of the plutocracy and likewise shared their rhetorical anti-Semitism. John Higham has called attention to a third anti-Semitic group of the nineties, the poorer classes in urban centers. Their prejudice cannot be described as merely verbal and rhetorical. Populists were not responsible for a protest signed by fourteen Jewish societies in 1899 that "no Jew can go on the street without exposing himself to the danger of being pitilessly beaten." That happened in Brooklyn, and the mob of 1902 that injured some two hundred people, mostly Jewish, went into action in Lower East Side New York.

Populist anti-Semitism is not to be excused on the ground that it was verbal, nor dismissed because the prejudice received more violent expression in urban quarters. But all will admit that the charge of anti-Semitism has taken on an infinitely more ominous and hideous significance since the Nazi genocide furnaces than it ever had before, at least in Anglo-American society. The Populists' use of the Shylock symbol was not wholly innocent, but they used it as a folk stereotype, and little had happened in the Anglo-Saxon community between the time of Shakespeare and that of the Populists which burdened the latter with additional guilt in repeating the stereotype.

The South, again, was a special instance. Much had happened there to enhance the guilt of racist propaganda and to exacerbate racism. But anti-Semitism was not the trouble, and to stress it in connection with the South of the nineties would be comparable to stressing anti-Negro feeling in the Arab states of the Middle East today. Racism there was, in alarming quantity, but it was directed against another race, and it was not merely rhetorical. The Negro suffered far more discrimination and violence than the Jew did in that era or later. Moreover, there was little in the Southern tradition to restrain the political exploitation of anti-Negro prejudice and much more to encourage its use than there was in the American tradition with respect to anti-Semitism. Racism was exploited in the South with fantastic refinements and revolting excesses in the Populist period. Modern students of the dynamics of race prejudice find marked similarities between anti-Negro feelings and anti-Semitism and in the psychological traits of those to whom both appeal. First in the list of those traits under both anti-Negro attitudes and anti-Semitism is "the feeling of deprivation"; another, lower in the list but common to both, is "economic apprehensions." The Southern Populists would seem to have constituted the perfect market for Negrophobia.

But perhaps the most remarkable aspect of the whole Populist movement was the resistance its leaders in the South put up against racism and racist propaganda and the determined effort they made against incredible odds to win back political rights for the Negroes, defend those rights against brutal aggression, and create among their normally anti-Negro following, even temporarily, a spirit of tolerance in which the two races of the South could work together in one party for the achievement of common ends. These efforts included not only the defense of the Negro's right to vote but also his right to hold office, serve on juries, receive justice in the courts and defense against lynchers. The Populists failed, and some of them turned bitterly against the Negro as the cause of their failure. But in the efforts they made for racial justice and political rights they went further toward extending the Negro political fellowship, recognition, and equality than any native white political movement has ever gone before or since in the South. This record is of greater historical significance and deserves more emphasis and attention than any anti-Semitic tendencies the movement manifested in that region or any other. If resistance to racism is the test of acceptability for a place in the American political heritage, Populism would seem to deserve more indulgence at the hands of its critics than it has recently enjoyed.

Two other aspects of identification between the old Populism and the New Radical Right require critical modification. Talcott Parsons, Max Lerner, and Victor Ferkiss, among others, find that the old regional strongholds of Populism tended to become the strongholds of isolationism in the period between the two world wars and believe there is more than a fortuitous connection between a regional proneness to Populism and isolationism. These and other critics believe also that they discern a logical connection between a regional addiction to Populism in the old days and to McCarthyism in recent times.

In both of these hypotheses the critics have neglected to take into account the experience of the South and mistakenly assumed a strong Populist heritage in the Middle West. Although one of the strongest centers of Populism, if not the strongest, the South in the foreign policy crisis before the Second World War was the least isolationist and the most internationalist and interventionist part of the country. After the war, according to Nathan Glazer and Seymour Lipset, who base their statement on opinion poll studies, "the South was the most anti-McCarthy section of the country." It is perfectly possible that in rejecting isolationism and McCarthyism the South was "right" for the "wrong" reasons, traditional and historical reasons. V. O. Key has suggested that among the reasons for its position on foreign policy were centuries of dependence on world trade, the absence of any concentration of Irish or Germanic population, and the predominantly British origin of the white population. Any adequate explanation of the South's rejection of McCarthy would be complex, but part of it might be the region's peculiarly rich historical experience with its own assortment of demagogues—Populistic and other varieties—and the consequent acquirement of some degree of sophistication and some minimal standards of decency in the arts of demagoguery. No one has attempted to explain the South's anti-isolationism and anti-McCarthyism by reference to its Populist heritage—and certainly no such explanation is advanced here.

To do justice to the new critique of Populism it should be acknowledged that much of its bill of indictment is justified. It is true that the Populists were a provincial lot and that much of their thinking was provincial. It is true that they took refuge in the agrarian myth, that they denied the commercial character of agricultural enterprise and sometimes dreamed of a Golden Age. In their economic thought they overemphasized the importance of money and oversimplified the nature of their problems by claiming a harmony of interest between farmer and labor, by dividing the world into "producers" and "nonproducers," by reducing all conflict to "just two sides," and by thinking that too many ills and too many remedies of the world were purely legislative. Undoubtedly many of them were fascinated with the notion of conspiracy and advanced conspiratorial theories of history, and some of them were given to apocalyptic premonitions of direful portent.

To place these characteristics in perspective, however, one should enquire how many of them are peculiar to the Populists and how many are shared by the classes, or groups, or regions, or by the period to which the Populists belong. The great majority of Populists were provincial, ill-educated, and rural, but so were the great majority of Americans in the nineties, Republicans and Democrats as well. They were heir to all the superstition, folklore, and prejudice that is the heritage of the ill-informed. The Populists utilized and institutionalized some of this, but so did their opponents. There were a good many conspiratorial theories, economic nostrums, and oversimplifications adrift in the latter part of the nineteenth century, and the Populists had no monopoly of them. They did overemphasize the importance of money, but scarcely more so than did their opponents, the Gold Bugs. The preoccupation with monetary reforms and remedies was a characteristic of the period rather than a peculiarity of the Populists. The genuine Populist, moreover, was more concerned with the "primacy of credit" than with the "primacy of money," and his insistence that the federal government was the only agency powerful enough to provide a solution for the agricultural credit problem proved to be sound. So did his contention that the banking system was stacked against his interest and that reform in this field was overdue.

The Populist doctrine of a harmony of interest between farmer and labor, between workers and small businessmen, and the alignment of these "producers" against the parasitic "nonproducers" is not without precedent in our political history. Any party that aspires to gain power in America must strive for a coalition of conflicting interest groups. The Populist effort was no more irrational in this respect than was the Whig coalition and many others, including the New Deal.

The political crises of the nineties evoked hysterical responses and apocalyptic delusions in more than one quarter. Excesses of the leaders of a protest movement of provincial, unlettered, and angry farmers are actually more excusable and understandable than the rather similar responses of the spokesmen of the educated, successful, and privileged classes of the urban East. There would seem to be less excuse for hysteria and conspiratorial obsessions among the latter. One thinks of the *Nation* describing the

Sherman Silver Purchase Act as a "socialistic contrivance of gigantic proportions," of J. Laurence Laughlin writing of "the great silver conspiracy" in the *Atlantic Monthly* of 1896, or of Police Commissioner Theodore Roosevelt declaring in "the greatest soberness" that the Populists were "plotting a social revolution and the subversion of the American Republic" and proposing to make an example of twelve of their leaders by "shooting them dead" against a wall. There was Joseph H. Choate before the Supreme Court pronouncing the income tax "the beginnings of socialism and communism" and "the destruction of the Constitution itself." For violence of rhetoric *Harper's Weekly,* the *Atlantic Monthly,* the New York *Tribune,* and the Springfield *Republican* could hold their own with the wool-hat press in the campaign of 1896. Hysteria was not confined to mugwump intellectuals with status problems. Mark Hanna told an assembly of his wealthy friends at the Union League Club they were acting like "a lot of scared hens."

Anarchism was almost as much a conspiracy symbol for conservatives as Wall Street was for the Populists, and conservatives responded to any waving of the symbol even more irrationally, for there was less reality in the menace of anarchism for capitalism. John Hay had a vituperative address called "The Platform of Anarchy" that he used in the campaign of 1896. The Springfield *Republican* called Bryan "the exaltation of anarchy"; Dr. Lyman Abbott labeled Bryanites "the anarchists of the Northwest," and Dr. Charles H. Parkhurst was excited about the menace of "anarchism" in the Democratic platform. It was the

Populist sympathizer, Governor John Peter Altgeld of Illinois, who pardoned the three anarchists of Haymarket, victims of conservative hysteria, and who partly corrected the gross miscarriage of justice that had resulted in the hanging of four others. The New York *Times* promptly denounced Governor Altgeld as a secret anarchist himself, and Theodore Roosevelt said that Altgeld would conspire to inaugurate "a red government of lawlessness and dishonesty as fantastic and vicious as the Paris Commune." There was more than a touch of conspiratorial ideology in the desperate conservative reaction to the agrarian revolt. An intensive study of the nineties can hardly fail to leave the impression that this decade had rather more than its share of zaniness and crankiness and that these qualities were manifested in the higher and middling as well as the lower orders of American society.

Venturing beyond the 1890's and speaking of populists with a small "p," some of the new critics would suggest that popular protest movements of the populistic style throughout our history have suffered from a peculiar addiction to scares, scapegoats, and conspiratorial notions. It is true that such movements tend to attract the less sophisticated, the people who are likely to succumb to cranks and the appeal of their menaces, and conspiratorial obsessions. But before one accepts this as a populistic or radical peculiarity, one should recall that the Jacobin Scare of the 1790's was a Federalist crusade and that the populistic elements of that era were its victims and not its perpetrators. One should remember also that A. Mitchell Palmer and the superpatriots who staged the Great Red Scare of 1919–1920 were not populistic in their outlook. One of the most successful conspiratorial theories of history in American politics was the "Great Slave Conspiracy" notion advanced by the abolitionists and later incorporated in the Republican party credo for several decades.

Richard Hofstadter has put his finger on a neglected tendency of some Populists and Progressives as well, the tendency he calls "deconversion from reform to reaction," the tendency to turn cranky, illiberal, and sour. This happened with disturbing frequency among leaders as well as followers of Populism. Perhaps the classic example is the Georgia Populist, Tom Watson, twice his party's candidate for President and once for Vice President. When Watson soured he went the whole way. By no means all of the Populist leaders turned sour, and there has been an overemphasis on a handful of stock examples, but there are several valid instances. Even more disturbing is the same tendency to turn sour among the old Populist rank and file, to take off after race phobias, religious hatreds, and witch hunts. The reasons for this retrograde tendency among reformers to embrace the forces they have spent years in fighting have not been sufficiently investigated. It may be that in some instances the reform movement appeals to personalities with unstable psychological traits. In the case of the Populists, however, it would seem that a very large part of the explanation lies in embittered frustration—repeated and tormenting frustration of both the leaders and the led.

Whatever the explanation, it cannot be denied that some of the offshoots of Populism are less than lovely to contemplate and rather painful to recall. Misshapen and sometimes hideous, they are caricatures of the Populist ideal, though their kinship with the genuine article is undeniable. No one in his right mind can glory in their memory, and it would at times be a welcome relief to renounce the whole Populist heritage in order to be rid of the repulsive aftermath. Repudiation of the Populist tradition presents the liberal-minded Southerner in particular with a temptation of no inconsiderable appeal, for it would unburden him of a number of embarrassing associations.

In his study of populist traits in American society, Edward Shils has some perceptive observations on the difficult relations between politicians and intellectuals. He adds a rather wistful footnote: "How painful the American situation looked to our intellectuals when they thought of Great Britain. There the cream of the graduates of the two ancient universities entered the civil service by examinations which were delightfully archaic and which had no trace of spoils patronage about them. . . . Politics, radical politics, conducted in a seemly fashion by the learned and reflective was wonderful. It was an ideal condition which was regretfully recognized as impossible to reproduce in the United States." He himself points out many of the reasons why this is possible in Britain, the most dignified member of the parliamentary fraternity: respect for "betters," mutual trust within the ruling classes, deferential attitudes of working class and middle class, the aura of aristocracy and monarchy that still suffuses the institutions of a government no longer aristocratic, the retention of the status and the symbols of hierarchy despite economic leveling. No wonder that from some points of view "the British system seemed an intellectual's paradise."

America has it worse—or at least different. The deferential attitude lingers only in the South, and there mainly as a quaint gesture of habit. Respect for "betters" is un-American. Glaring publicity replaces mutual trust as the *modus vivendi* among the political elite. No aura of aristocratic decorum and hierarchal sanctity surrounds our governmental institutions, even the most august of them. Neither Supreme Court nor State Department nor Army is immune from popular assault and the rude hand of suspicion. The sense of institutional identity is weak, and so are institutional loyalties. Avenues between the seats of learning and the seats of power are often blocked by mistrust and mutual embarrassment.

America has no reason to expect that it could bring off a social revolution without a breach of decorum or the public peace, nor that the revolutionary party would eventually be led by a graduate of exclusive Winchester and Oxford. American politics are not ordinarily "conducted in a seemly fashion by the learned and reflective." Such success as we have enjoyed in this respect—the instances of the Sage of Monticello and the aristocrat of Hyde Park come to mind—have to be accounted for by a large element of luck. Close investigation of popular upheavals of protest and reform in the political history of the United States has increasingly revealed of late that they have all had their seamy side and their share of the irrational, the zany, and the retrograde. A few of the more successful movements have borrowed historical reputability from the memory of the worthies who led them, but others have not been so fortunate either in their leaders or their historians.

One must expect and even hope that there will be future upheavals to shock the seats of power and privilege and furnish the periodic therapy that seems necessary to the health of our democracy. But one cannot expect them to be any more decorous or seemly or rational than their predecessors. One can reasonably hope, however, that they will not all fall under the sway of the Huey Longs and Father Coughlins who will be ready to take charge. Nor need they, if the tradition is maintained which enabled a Henry George to place himself at the vanguard of the antimonopoly movement in his day, which encouraged a Henry Demarest Lloyd to labor valiantly to shape the course of Populism, or which prompted an Upton Sinclair to try to make sense of a rag-tag-and-bob-tail aberration in California.

For the tradition to endure, for the way to remain open, however, the intellectual must not be alienated from the sources of revolt. It was one of the glories of the New Deal that it won the support of the intellectual and one of the tragedies of Populism that it did not. The intellectual must resist the impulse to identify all the irrational and evil forces he detests with such movements because some of them, or the aftermath or epigone of some of them, have proved so utterly repulsive. He will learn all he can from the new criticism about the irrational and illiberal side of Populism and other reform movements, but he cannot afford to repudiate the heritage.

8

The Irony of Southern History

IN A TIME WHEN NATIONALISM SWEEPS EVERYTHING ELSE
before it, as it does at present, the regional historian is
likely to be oppressed by a sense of his unimportance.
America is the all-important subject, and national ideas,
national institutions, and national policies are the themes
that compel attention. Foreign peoples, eager to know
what this New-World colossus means to them and their
immediate future, are impatient with details of regional
variations, and Americans, intent on the need for national
unity, tend to minimize their importance. New England,
the West, and other regions are occasionally permitted to
speak for the nation. But the South is thought to be hedged
about with peculiarities that set it apart as unique. As a
standpoint from which to write American history it is
regarded as eccentric and, as a background for an historian,
something of a handicap to be overcome.

Of the eccentric position of the South in the nation there
are admittedly many remaining indications. I do not think,
however, that this eccentricity need be regarded as entirely

a handicap. In fact, I think that it could possibly be turned to advantage by the Southern historian, both in understanding American history and in interpreting it to non-Americans. For from a broader point of view it is not the South but America that is unique among the peoples of the world. This peculiarity arises out of the American legend of success and victory, a legend that is not shared by any other people of the civilized world. The collective will of this country has simply never known what it means to be confronted by complete frustration. Whether by luck, by abundant resources, by ingenuity, by technology, by organizing cleverness, or by sheer force of arms America has been able to overcome every major historic crisis—economic, political, or foreign—with which it has had to cope. This remarkable record has naturally left a deep imprint upon the American mind. It explains in large part the national faith in unlimited progress, in the efficacy of material means, in the importance of mass and speed, the worship of success, and the belief in the invincibility of American arms.

The legend has been supported by an unbroken succession of victorious wars. Battles have been lost, and whole campaigns—but not wars. In the course of their national history Americans, who have been called a bellicose though unmartial people, have fought eight wars, and so far without so much as one South African fiasco such as England encountered in the heyday of her power. This unique good fortune has isolated America, I think rather dangerously, from the common experience of the rest of mankind, all the great peoples of which have without exception known the bitter taste of defeat and humiliation. It has fostered the tacit conviction that American ideals, values, and principles inevitably prevail in the end. That conviction has never received a name, nor even so much explicit formulation as the old concept of Manifest Destiny. It is assumed, not discussed. And the assumption exposes us to the temptation of believing that we are somehow immune from the forces of history.

The country that has come nearest to approximating the American legend of success and victory is England. The nearness of continental rivals and the precariousness of the balance of power, however, bred in the English an historical sophistication that prevented the legend from flourishing as luxuriantly as it has in the American climate. Only briefly toward the end of the Victorian period did the legend threaten to get out of hand in England. Arnold J. Toynbee has recalled those piping days in a reminiscent passage. "I remember watching the Diamond Jubilee procession myself as a small boy," he writes. "I remember the atmosphere. It was: well, here we are on the top of the world, and we have arrived at this peak to stay there—forever! There is, of course, a thing called history, but history is something unpleasant that happens to other people. We are comfortably outside all that. I am sure, if I had been a small boy in New York in 1897 I should have felt the same. Of course, if I had been a small boy in 1897 in the Southern part of the United States, I should not have felt the same; I should then have known from my parents that history had happened to my people in my part of the world."

The South has had its full share of illusions, fantasies, and pretensions, and it has continued to cling to some of them with an astonishing tenacity that defies explanation. But the illusion that "history is something unpleasant that happens to other people" is certainly not one of them—not in the face of accumulated evidence and memory to the contrary. It is true that there have been many Southern converts to the gospel of progress and success, and there was even a period following Reconstruction when it seemed possible that these converts might carry a reluctant region with them. But the conversion was never anywhere near complete. Full participation in the legend of irresistible progress, success, and victory could, after all, only be vicarious at best. For the inescapable facts of history were that the South had repeatedly met with frustration and failure. It had learned what it was to be faced with economic, social, and political problems that refused to yield to all the ingenuity, patience, and intelligence that a people could bring to bear upon them. It had learned to accommodate itself to conditions that it swore it would never accept, and it had learned the taste left in the mouth by the swallowing of one's own words. It had learned to live for long decades in quite un-American poverty, and it had learned the equally un-American lesson of submission. For the South had undergone an experience that it could share with no other part of America—though it is shared by nearly all the peoples of Europe and Asia—the experience of military defeat, occupation, and reconstruction.

Nothing about this history was conducive to the theory that the South was the darling of divine providence.

2

In his book, *The Irony of American History,* Reinhold Niebuhr conducts an astute analysis of national character and destiny that emphasizes another set of American pretensions, which he calls the illusions of innocence and virtue. These illusions have their origins in both North and South, though at a period before there was any distinct regional consciousness. They were fostered by the two great moral traditions of early national life, New England Calvinism and Virginia deism of the Jeffersonian school. While they differed upon theology, theocrats and deists were agreed that their country was "God's American Israel," called out of a wicked and corrupt Old World and set apart by Providence to create a new humanity and restore man's lost innocence. I believe that Niebuhr would agree that what I have described as the American legend of success and victory has assisted in fostering and perpetuating these illusions of innocence and virtue. At any rate he demonstrates that these illusions have been preserved past infancy and into national adulthood. Arriving at man's estate, we have suddenly found ourselves in possession of immense and undreamed of power and compelled to use this power in ways that are not innocent and that cover us with guilt. In clinging to our infant illusions of innocence along with our new power, writes the theologian, we are "involved in ironic perils which compound the experiences of Babylon and Israel"—the perils of overweening power and overweening virtue.

Our opposite numbers in the world crisis, the Russian Communists, are bred on illusions of innocence and virtue that parallel our own with ironic fidelity, even though they are of very different origin and have been used to disguise (perhaps even from themselves) what seems to us much greater guilt of oppression and cruelty. They combine these illusions with Messianic passions that find a paler reflection in one layer of American conscience. Looking upon their own nation as the embodiment of innocence and justice, the Russians take it for granted that America is the symbol of the worst form of capitalistic injustice. Both America and Russia find it almost impossible to believe that anyone could think ill of them and are persuaded that only malice could prompt suspicions of motives so obviously virtuous. Each tends to regard the other as the only force wilfully thwarting its dream of bringing happiness to all mankind.

There are many perils, both for our nation and for the world, inherent in this situation—and they do not all come from abroad. We are exasperated by the ironic incongruities of our position. Having more power than ever before, America ironically enjoys less security than in the days of her weakness. Convinced of her virtue, she finds that even her allies accuse her of domestic vices invented by her enemies. The liberated prove ungrateful for their liberation, the reconstructed for their reconstruction, and the late colonial peoples vent their resentment upon our nation—the most innocent, we believe, of the imperial powers. Driven by these provocations and frustrations, there is the danger that America may be tempted to exert all the terrible power she possesses to compel history to conform to her own illusions. The extreme, but by no means the only expression, would be the so-called preventive war. This would be to commit the worst heresy of the Marxists, with whom it is dogma that they can compel history to conform to the pattern of their dreams by the ruthless use of force.

To save ourselves from these moral perils, Dr. Niebuhr adjures us to disavow the pretensions and illusions of innocence derived from our national childhood, along with all self-righteousness, complacency, and humorless idealism. If we would understand our plight and prepare for the role we must play, we must grasp the ironic implications of our history. I realize that Niebuhr's view of human strivings is based on theology, a subject definitely beyond my province. Whatever its theological implications—and I have frankly never explored them—the view has a validity apart from them that appeals to the historian. Yet the ironic interpretation of history is rare and difficult. In the nature of things the participants in an ironic situation are rarely conscious of the irony, else they would not become its victims. Awareness must ordinarily be contributed by an observer, a nonparticipant, and the observer must have an unusual combination of detachment and sympathy. He must be able to appreciate both elements in the incongruity that go to make up the ironic situation, both the virtue and the vice to which pretensions of virtue lead. He must not be so hostile as to deny the element of virtue or strength on the one side, nor so sympathetic as to ignore the vanity and weakness to which the virtue and strength have contributed. Obviously, the qualifications of the ironic historian are pretty hard to come by.

3

Now the South is deeply involved at present in the ironic plight of our country as a full-fledged participant. In fact, the headlong precipitancy with which the South has responded to the slogans of nationalism in recent world crises has often exceeded that of other sections of the country. Mass response sometimes suggests the zeal of recent converts. Yet there are aspects of its history and experience that make the South an observer as well as a participant, which set it apart in certain ways from the experience of the rest of the country, and which constitute a somewhat detached point of view. From that vantage point I believe it is possible for the Southern historian, and indeed all those absorbed in the study of Southern history, to make a special contribution to the understanding of the irony of American history, as well as that of the South's history.

Ironic implications of Southern history are not concealed by any legend of success and victory nor by the romantic legend of the Lost Cause. To savor the full irony of the confident and towering ante-bellum dream of a Greek Democracy for the New World one has only to recall the words of a speech that Robert Barnwell Rhett made when

South Carolina seceded. The orator was picturing the historian of 2000 A.D. writing this passage: "And extending their empire across this continent to the Pacific, and down through Mexico to the other side of the great gulf, and over the isles of the sea, they established an empire and wrought out a civilization which has never been equalled or surpassed—a civilization teeming with orators, poets, philosophers, statesmen, and historians equal to those of Greece and Rome—and presented to the world the glorious spectacle of a free, prosperous, and illustrious people." As a matter of fact, in the eyes of the true believer the coming of the Golden Age did not have to await the year 2000. It had already arrived, full blown, here and now. For as Charles Sydnor has observed, "the affirmation of Southern perfection" meant just that. Blind to evils and imperfections all around them, Southerners described what they saw as the ultimate in social perfection. "Fighting to defend their way of life," says Sydnor, "they had taken refuge in a dream world, and they insisted that others accept their castle in the sky as an accurate description of conditions in the South."

The shattering of this dream and the harsh education that followed has not made the South the home of a race of philosophers. Nor does it seem to have made Southerners any wiser than their fellow countrymen. But it has provided them with a different point of view from which they might, if they will, judge and understand their own history and American history, and from which to view the ironic plight of modern America.

The meaning of the contrast between the 1930's and

the 1940's is a case in point. This transformation took place too recently for anyone to have forgotten, though many seem to have forgotten it entirely. In the thirties and well into the following decade there occurred the most thoroughgoing inquest of self-criticism that our national economy has ever undergone—not even excepting that of the muckraking and progressive era. No corner nor aspect nor relationship of American capitalism was overlooked, and no shibboleth of free enterprise went unchallenged. The prying and probing went on at every level from the share croppers to holding companies and international cartels. Subpoenas brought mighty bankers and public utility empire-builders to the witness stand. Nor was this activity merely the work of the wild-eyed and the woolly-haired, nor the exclusive concern of one of the major parties. It was a popular theme of the radio, the press, the screen, the theater, and even the pulpit. Some churches took up the theme and incorporated it into their programs. Universities hummed and throbbed with it. And in 1940 the former president of a public utility holding company, then candidate for President of the United States on the Republican ticket, made the theme a part of his campaign. Some of the outpouring of criticism in the thirties and forties was misdirected, some was perhaps a bit silly. But the electorate repeatedly endorsed with large majorities the party that was the more closely identified with the movement. On the whole, the people regarded it as productive of good. It was at least indicative of a healthy and self-confident society, uninhibited by fear.

Then in the mid-forties something happened. It happened rather suddenly. The floodstream of criticism dwindled to a trickle and very nearly ceased altogether. It was as if some giant sluice gate had been firmly shut. The silence that followed was soon filled with the clamor of voices lifted in accusation, denial, or recantation. No reputation was now secure from the charges of the heresy hunters, the loyalty investigators, and the various committees on public orthodoxy and conformity. Choruses were lifted in rapturous praise of the very institutions that had been so recently the objects of attack—and the choruses were joined by many of the former critics.

Surveying this remarkable transformation, the historian of the South can hardly escape the feeling that all this has happened before—or something strongly suggestive of it: that what happened in the 1940's had its counterpart in the 1830's. The earlier development was on a smaller scale, to be sure, and there were certain other obvious discrepancies to be taken into account. The dangers inherent in any such comparison between historical epochs are numerous and forbidding, for certainly no analogy is perfect since no two eras, movements, nor events are entirely alike. To suggest that modern capitalism is comparable with slavery as a system of labor would be to indulge in the loose and irresponsible language of polemics and propaganda. With due precaution and full awareness of the risks, however, one may venture a comparison, not between the two institutions, but between the public attitudes toward them and the transformations that took place in those attitudes.

What happened in the South during the 1830's is too

familiar a story to require elaboration here. Before it happened, however, we know that the Jeffersonian tradition protected and fostered a vigorous school of antislavery thought in the South. The great Virginians of the Revolutionary generation, nearly all of whom were on record for emancipation, lent their prestige to the movement. Critics of slavery spared no aspect of the peculiar institution. They spoke out against the effect on the master as well as on the slave; they exposed the harm done the manners and morals of the South as well as its economy and society. Nor were critics mere misfits and radicals. They included men of influence and standing—politicians, editors, professors, and clergymen. Antislavery thought appeared in respectable newspapers and infiltrated evangelical sects of the Upper South particularly. In the 1820's the slave states contained a great many more antislavery societies than the free states and furnished leadership for the movement in the country. It would be false to suggest that slavery was on the way out, or, in spite of some amelioration, that the reformers made any very substantial alterations. But it is not too much to say that this was a society unafraid of facing its own evils. The movement reached a brilliant climax in the free and full debates over emancipation in the Virginia legislature during the session of 1831–1832. The effort to abolish slavery failed there as elsewhere. But as Joseph Roberts writes, "The institution was denounced as never before; it was condemned wholesale fashion by legal representatives of a slave-holding people. The vigor and breadth of the assault provide the debate with its most obvious distinction."

In spite of the vigor of the movement and the depth of
its root in Southern tradition, it withered away to almost
nothing in a very brief period during the middle thirties.
By 1837 there was not one antislavery society remaining
in the whole South. Of the thousands of voices that had
been raised in outspoken protest a short while before there
were to be heard only a few whispers. Opponents changed
their opinions or held their tongues. Loyalty to the South
came to be defined in terms of conformity of thought regarding one of its institutions. Past records and associates
were scrutinized closely, and the recency with which one
had denounced Northern abolitionism became a matter
of public concern. The South concentrated its energies
upon the repression of heresy and raised intellectual barricades against the ideas of a critical and unfriendly world.
The institution that had so recently been blamed for a mul-
titude of the region's ills was now pictured as the secret of
its superiority and the reason for its fancied perfection.

4

Causes behind the transformation of attitudes in the
South were numerous and complex. So are the reasons
behind the transformation that has taken place in the attitudes of contemporary America. Broadly speaking, however, both of these revolutions in public attitudes were reactions to contests for power in which the two societies
found themselves involved. These great struggles included
many clashes of interest and issues quite apart from those

concerning morals and contrasting labor systems. Even in the absence of ideological differences the strains of conflict would have been severe in each case. In the 1850's as in the 1950's, however, the crisis tended to be increasingly dramatized as a clash between different systems of labor—as slave labor versus free labor. In both the nineteenth-century war of words and the twentieth-century cold war each party to the conflict, of course, contended that the other practiced the more immoral, wicked, and shameless type of exploitation and that its own system was benevolent, idealistic, and sound. Our own opinions as to which of the parties in each crisis was the more deluded or disingenuous in its contentions are likely to be pretty firmly fixed already, and the problem is such that it need not detain us.

The point is that there exists, in spite of obvious differences, a disquieting suggestion of similarity between the two crises and the pattern of their development. The mistakes of the South, some of which have already been suggested, are readily apparent and their meaning open to all who would read and understand. In the first place the South permitted the opposition to define the issue, and naturally the issue was not defined to the South's advantage. In the second place the South assumed the moral burden of proof. Because the attack centered upon slavery, the defense rallied around that point. As the clamor increased and the emotional pitch of the dispute intensified, the South heedlessly allowed its whole cause, its way of life, its traditional values, and its valid claims in numerous

nonmoral disputes with the North to be identified with
one institution—and that an institution of which the South
itself had furnished some of the most intelligent critics.
It was a system known to have reached the natural limits
of its expansion in this country already and one which was
far gone on its way to abandonment abroad. Yet, in its
quest for friends and allies, the South made the mistake
of competing with the North for the favor of the West by
insisting upon the acceptance of a system totally unadapted
to the conditions and needs of the territories and often
offensive to their moral sensibilities. And in looking to
Europe for support from England and France, powers that
might reasonably have been expected to be drawn to its
cause for reasons of self-interest, the South encountered
difficulties from the start. Some, though certainly not all,
of these difficulties were due to the fact that those countries had already repudiated the system upon which the
South had elected to stand or fall.

The knowledge that it was rapidly being isolated in the
world community as the last champion of an outmoded
system under concerted moral attack contributed to the
South's feeling of insecurity and its conviction that it was
being encircled and menaced from all sides. In place of
its old eagerness for new ideas and its out-going com-
municativeness the South developed a suspicious inhos-
pitality toward the new and the foreign, a tendency to withdraw from what it felt to be a critical world. Because it
identified the internal security of the whole society with
the security of its labor system, it refused to permit criti-

cism of that system. To guarantee conformity of thought it abandoned its tradition of tolerance and resorted to repression of dissent within its borders and to forceful exclusion of criticism from outside. And finally it set about to celebrate, glorify, and render all but sacrosanct with praise the very institution that was under attack and that was responsible for the isolation and insecurity of the South.

Modern America is more fortunate than the ante bellum South in having an economic system which, though threatened with abandonment by other countries, has shown few of the serious weaknesses and is covered with little of the moral obloquy from which slavery suffered. And in spite of verbal orthodoxy regarding the doctrine of capitalistic free enterprise, the American political genius has shown willingness to experiment extensively with heterodox cures for ills of the orthodox system. This experimentation has, of course, been accompanied by loud protests of loyalty to the true faith. Again, modern America is not inherently nor necessarily handicapped in the struggle against its powerful antagonist by all the weaknesses that helped to doom the South to defeat.

There is, however, no cause for complacency in this good fortune. Nor does it rule out entirely the analogy that is here suggested. We should not deceive ourselves about the opinions of other peoples. While we see ourselves as morally sound and regard our good fortune as the natural and just reward of our soundness, these views are not shared by large numbers of people in many parts of the world.

They look on our great wealth not as the reward of our virtue but as proof of our wickedness, as evidence of the ruthless exploitation, not only of our own working people but of themselves. For great masses of people who live in abject poverty and know nothing firsthand of our system or of industrialism of any kind are easily persuaded that their misery is due to capitalist exploitation rather than to the shortcomings of their own economies. Hundreds of millions of these people are taught to believe that we are as arrogant, brutal, immoral, ruthless, and wicked as ever the South was pictured in an earlier war of words. Among their leaders are extremists ready with the conclusion that people so wicked do not deserve to live and that any means whatever used to destroy their system is justified by the end. One of these means is the subversive indoctrination of our labor force for insurrection. The malevolent caricature of our society contrasts so glaringly with what we believe to be the demonstrable facts—not to mention the contrast with our traditional illusions of virtue and inno-cence—that we are driven to indignation. And when we hear faint echoes of the same propaganda from our own allies, who no longer share our dedication to capitalism, our indignation turns into a sense of outrage.

Fortunately modern America has not yet followed the course of the South between 1830 and 1860, but the pattern of response evoked by these exasperations is not a wholly unfamiliar one. There are some unhappy similarities. Threatened with isolation as the last important defender of an economic system that has been abandoned or rejected without a trial by most of the world and that is under constant moral attack from several quarters, we have rallied to the point of attack. We have showed a tendency to allow our whole cause, our traditional values, and our way of life to be identified with one economic institution. Some of us have also tended to identify the security of the country with the security of that institution. We have swiftly turned from a mood of criticism to one of glorifying the institution as the secret of our superiority. We have showed a strong disposition to suppress criticism and repel outside ideas. We have been tempted to define loyalty as conformity of thought, and to run grave risk of moral and intellectual stultification.

Opposing each of these dangerous tendencies there is still healthy and wholesome resistance struggling to reassert our ancient tradition of tolerance and free criticism, to maintain balance and a sense of humor, to repel the temptation of self-righteousness and complacency, and to reject the fallacy that the whole American cause and tradition must stand or fall with one economic dogma. But it is too early to say that on any one of these points the healthy resistance is certain of triumph. In fact the fight is uphill, and in many instances the issue is doubtful. I am not contending that successful resistance to all the tendencies I have deplored will guarantee peace and solve the problems that plagued the 1950's, any more than I am sure that the same course would have resulted as happily in the 1850's. But I believe I am safe in contending that, in view of the South's experience, each of these tendencies should be the subject of gravest concern.

5

In the field of diplomacy and foreign relations modern America suffers from a divided mind, torn between one policy that is reminiscent of the way of the South and another more suggestive of the way of the North in the Civil War crisis. On the one hand are those who would meet the foreign challenge by withdrawing from a critical community of nations teeming with heresies and, by erecting an impregnable barricade, forcibly keep out all alien ways, influences, and ideas. Another modern group that has a counterpart in at least one school of Southerners in the 1850's are those who in the 1960's, heedless of world opinion, would brook no opposition, would not co-operate with, nor consult, other people's views, but insist that America must be strong enough to carry her way by economic coercion or by force. Suggestive also of the Southern way are those who, in competing with our opponents for the favor of uncommitted peoples, would urge upon them institutions and abstract ideas of our own that have little or no relevance to their real needs and circumstances. There are those who resent as evidence of disloyalty any defection on the part of our allies from the particular economic faith upon which we have decided to take our stand.

More reminiscent of the way of the North, on the other hand, are those who hold that this is an irrepressible conflict, that a world divided against itself cannot stand, that the issue is essentially a moral one, that we are morally obliged to liberate the enslaved peoples of the earth, punish the wicked oppressors, and convert the liberated peoples to our way of thought. The true American mission, according to those who support this view, is a moral crusade on a world-wide scale. Such people are likely to concede no validity whatever and grant no hearing to the opposing point of view, and to appeal to a higher law to justify bloody and revolting means in the name of a noble end. For what end could be nobler, they ask, than the liberation of man? Fortunately wiser counsel has generally prevailed, counsel which has charted a course of foreign policy between the perilous extremes of isolationism and world crusade. But each of the extreme courses still has powerful advocates, and neither can yet be regarded as a dead issue.

We have been admonished lately to heed the ironic consequences of the characteristic American approach to international affairs since the beginning of the present century. The main deficiencies of our policy of the last fifty years, we are told, are our legalistic and moralistic approaches to foreign relations. It is possible and even desirable, I believe, to accept the validity of this critical insight without embracing the strictly amoral, pragmatic, power-conscious policy of national self-interest that has been proposed as an alternative by those who criticize the moralistic approach. It is all too apparent that the association of the legalistic with the moralistic concept results in a torrent of indignation and bitterness against the lawbreaker and a blinding conviction of moral superiority to the enemy. Expressed in military policy and war aims these passions overwhelm reason and find no bounds short of complete submission, unconditional surrender, and total domination of the defeated people. The irony of the moralistic approach, when exploited by nationalism, is that the high motive to end injustice and immorality actually results in making war more amoral and horrible than ever and in shattering the foundations of the political and moral order upon which peace has to be built.

There would appear to be valid grounds for seeking the origins of our moralistic aberrations in the period of the Civil War. While both sides to that dispute indulged in legalistic as well as moralistic pretensions, it was the South that was predominantly legalistic and the North that was overwhelmingly moralistic in its approach. Although Southern historians have made important contributions to the understanding of that crisis, it is doubtful whether anyone has stated more aptly the ironic consequence of the moralistic approach than a Northern historian. "Yankees went to war," writes Kenneth Stampp, "animated by the highest ideals of the nineteenth-century middle classes. . . . But what the Yankees achieved— for their generation at least—was a triumph not of middle-class ideals but of middle-class vices. The most striking products of their crusade were the shoddy aristocracy of the North and the ragged children of the South. Among the masses of Americans there were no victors, only the vanquished."

Ironic contrasts between noble purposes and sordid results, between idealistic aims and pragmatic consequences, are characteristic of reconstruction periods as well as war crises. This is nowhere more readily apparent than in the postwar period through which we have recently lived and with the problems of which we are still struggling. It is especially in such times that moralistic approaches and high-minded war aims come home to roost. As usual, it is only after the zeal of wartime idealism has spent itself that the opportunity is gained for realizing the ideals for which the war has been fought. When the idealistic aims are then found to be in conflict with selfish and pragmatic ends, it is the ideals that are likely to be sacrificed. The probability of moral confusion in reconstruction policy is increased when a nation finds itself called on to gird for a new world moral crusade before the reconstruction consequent upon the last is fairly launched. Opportunities for moral confusion are still further multiplied when the new crusade promises to be fought in alliance with the public enemies of the previous moral crusade and when the new enemy happens to have been an ally in the previous crusade.

Americans have in common the memories of an earlier experiment with reconstruction and are generally conscious of some of the shortcomings of that effort. But again, the South experienced that same historic episode from a somewhat different point of view. Once Southern historians have purged their minds of rancor and awakened out of a narrow parochialism they should be in a singularly strategic position to teach their fellow countrymen something of the pitfalls of radical reconstruction: of the disfranchisement of old ruling classes and the indoctrination of liberated peoples, of the occupation of conquered territory and the eradication of racial dogma, of the problems of reunion and the hazards of reaction. They should at least have a special awareness of the ironic incongruities between moral purpose and pragmatic result, of the way in which laudable aims of idealists can be perverted to sordid purposes, and of the readiness with which high-minded ideals can be forgotten.

With all her terrible power and new responsibilities, combined with her illusions of innocence and her legends of immunity from frustration and defeat, America stands in greater need than she ever did of understanding her own history. Our European friends, appalled by the impetuosity and naïveté of some of our deeds and assumptions, have attributed our lack of historical sophistication to our lack of a history—in their sense of the word. America's apparent immunity to the tragic and ironic aspects of man's fate—that charmed and fabled immunity that once made America the Utopia of both the common men and the philosophers of Europe—has come to be pictured as Europe's curse. For the fear that haunts Europeans is the fear that America's lack of a common basis of experience and suffering will blind her to the true nature of their dilemmas and end by plunging them into catastrophe. But the Europeans are not entirely right. America has a history. It is only that the tragic aspects and the ironic implications of that history have been obscured by the national legend of success and victory and by the perpetuation of infant illusions of innocence and virtue.

America has had cynical disparagement of her ideals

from foreign, unfriendly, or hostile critics. But she desperately needs criticism from historians of her own who can penetrate the legend without destroying the ideal, who can dispel the illusion of pretended virtue without denying the genuine virtues. Such historians must have learned that virtue has never been defined by national or regional boundaries, and that morality and rectitude are not the monopolies of factions or parties. They must reveal the fallacy of a diplomacy based on moral bigotry, as well as the fallacy of one that relies on economic coercion through the fancied indispensability of favored products. Their studies would show the futility of erecting intellectual barricades against unpopular ideas, of employing censorship and repression against social criticism, and of imposing the ideas of the conqueror upon defeated peoples by force of arms. Such historians would teach that economic systems, whatever their age, their respectability, or their apparent stability, are transitory and that any nation which elects to stand or fall upon one ephemeral institution has already determined its fate. The history they write would also constitute a warning that an overwhelming conviction in the righteousness of a cause is no guarantee of its ultimate triumph, and that the policy which takes into account the possibility of defeat is more realistic than one that assumes the inevitability of victory.

Such historians must have a rare combination of detachment and sympathy, and they must have established some measure of immunity from the fevers and prejudices of their own times, particularly those bred of nationalism, with all its myths and pretensions, and those born of hysteria that closes the mind to new ideas of all kinds. America might find such historians anywhere within her borders, North as well as South. But surely some of them might reasonably be expected to arise from that region where it is a matter of common knowledge that history has happened to their people in their part of the world.

Index